Batema

New Zealand Writer's HANDBOOK

Bateman

New Zealand Writer's HANDBOOK

5th Edition, fully revised and updated

An indispensable guide to getting published in New Zealand

David Bateman

Views expressed in this book are not necessarily those of David Bateman Ltd.

First published in 1990 by David Bateman Ltd,
30 Tarndale Grove, Albany, Auckland, New Zealand

Revised edition 1994
Revised edition 1998
Revised edition 2000
Revised edition 2002
Reprinted 2006
Reprinted 2007

ISBN: 978-1-86953-665-7

Design by Book Design Limited, Christchurch, New Zealand
Printed in China through Colorcraft Ltd., Hong Kong

Contents

1 Getting Started

New Zealand may have a small population by international standards, but it is a highly literate one. This fact is reflected in the abundance of books and magazines which fill our homes, workplaces, bookshops, newsagents, letterboxes and libraries. New Zealanders like to read and every word printed is written by someone.

Domestic circulation numbers are not always great — for example, a million seller in United States terms is equivalent to about 14,000 copies in New Zealand — but the range of tastes catered for is enormous. With all these words being written, rewritten, edited, printed, published, performed or broadcast there is ample scope for the freelance writer in New Zealand to carve his or her own niche in the market — perhaps not always a lucrative one, but one which should always bring rewards of one sort or another.

A wide range of books is available for beginners in the craft of writing, and although many are written for American or British markets, they are usually also of some use to the New Zealand novice. Scour your local library for books on writing and read them carefully. Tips and techniques for people who wish to start writing are fairly universal. Your library will have books about the craft of writing under the Dewey number 808. There are a number of good New Zealand titles that you may wish to consult for background information about writing, publishing and the media.

Some of the titles listed below are older titles that are out of print, but a good-sized public library should be able to locate them for you if they do not hold them in stock themselves:

BROMBY, R. & SANDER, J.B.
Getting Yourself Published: A Guide to Australia and New Zealand,
Sydney: Cromarty Press, 1985

BYKOFSKY, S. & SANDER, J.B.
The Complete Idiot's Guide to Getting Published,
New York, Alpha Books, 1998

COX, A., BURGESS, L. & MOHEKEY, S.
Writing and Presenting for Senior Students, Auckland: Longman, 1996

DUNSFORD, C.J.
Getting Published, The Inside Story: For NZ and International Writers,
Auckland–Frankfurt, Global Dialogues Press, 2006

EDWARDS, B.
How to Survive and Win with the Media: A Self-Defence Course for Interviewees,
Auckland: Tandem Press, 2000

GREENWOOD, R.
Writing, Auckland: Longman, 1996

GREVILLE, M.
Legal Research and Writing in New Zealand, Wellington: Butterworths, 2000

LEGAT, M.
Writing for a Living, London: A & C Black, 2000

NEALE, R.
The Common Writer: Theory and Practice for Writers and Teachers,
Oxford: Oxford University Press, 1991

NEALE, R. [ed.]
Writers on Writing: An Anthology, Oxford: Oxford University Press, 1992

OWEN, J.D.
Australian/New Zealand Guide to Writing and Selling Articles, Alexandria, NSW:
Hale and Iremonger, 1997

PRIESTLEY, B.
Investigative Reporting: A Beginner's Guide,
New Zealand Journalists Training Board, 1988

REYNOLDS, J.
Media Matter: A Practical Guide to New Zealand Media,
Auckland: Whitcoulls, 1984

ROGERS, A.
Write and Be Published: The Complete Guide to the Publication of Your Book,
Auckland: Reed, 1994

TREMEWAN, T. [ed.]
Write Edit Print: Style Manual for Aotearoa New Zealand,
Canberra: AGPS Press, 1997

ULLMANN, J.
Investigative Reporting: advanced methods and techniques,
New York: St Martin's Press, 1995

WAGEMAKER, P. [ed.]
Getting Into Print: Preparing Manuscripts for Publication,
Wellington: GP Books, 1990

ZACKHEIM, S.P. & Zackheim, A.
Getting Your Book Published for Dummies, New York: IDG, 2000

Although the best training for new writers is simply to write as much as they can, thus discovering new solutions to their own writing problems through practice and experience, there are many other avenues through which they can seek to improve their writing style and habits, and therefore their chances of success. There are various courses offered throughout the country. There are workshops and writers' groups in most areas, and organisations such as regional arts councils encourage new writers in various ways, for example through awards and competitions. If you are a novice writer, seek out as much information as you can about writing activities in your local area, and try to meet as many people as you can who are involved in writing.

Read, listen, practise, persevere — and after the usual rejection slips have arrived, keep waiting for that magical first acceptance letter!

Tools of the trade

Libraries

You can begin to write with nothing more than pen, paper and an idea but, sooner or later, there will come a time when these simple tools will no longer suffice.

Get to know your way around your nearest library, and aim to be familiar with all the resources it can give you, from books for research, New Zealand newspapers and periodicals for analysis, overseas publications for comparison, computer searches for material, Internet access, and interloan services for uncommon publications, down to more basic things like a photocopying machine or a quiet space when you have none at home.

Learn to use the electronic online catalogue or microfiche readers, and get to know where things are. Being able to go straight to the resource you need saves time and frustration.

The website www.nzlibraries.com offers connections to all the New Zealand public libraries that have websites. These sites offer a title search option, and many also have options for checking local library and community events. Most major libraries have comprehensive websites (see Chapter 3 for more information).

Libraries often feature community noticeboards too, and you should regularly consult these for occasional news of writing or publishing activities in your community.

Dictionaries

Dictionaries are essential accessories for even the most confident speller, and dozens of good ones are currently available. *The Concise Oxford Dictionary,* which includes American variations in spelling (useful for overseas submissions) is generally regarded as adequate for most needs. *The New Zealand Oxford Dictionary* is a large-scale dictionary with thousands of New Zealand-specific entries which many publications now use as a general style guide. It is also available in pocket and mini forms.

The *Oxford Dictionary for Writers and Editors* is a more specialised publication, containing a selection of the more tricky English words you may come up against. Collins puts out a *Concise Dictionary,* just as good in every respect as the Oxford version, and at about the same price; *Collins New Zealand Compact Dictionary* and *The New Zealand Pocket Oxford Dictionary* are also useful. Both publishers have a wide range of larger and smaller dictionaries to suit all needs (and pockets). A comprehensive and revised edition of *The Chambers Dictionary* is also available.

Penguin produces *The New Penguin English Dictionary* and Heinemann publishes the *Heinemann New Zealand Dictionary*. Another publication is the *Dictionary of New Zealand English,* published by Oxford University Press, which is a useful reference for New Zealand words and their origins. Also available are *The Reed Dictionary of Modern Maori* and the *English–Maori Dictionary* by H.M. Ngata.

Dictionaries and other reference works are often sold at reduced prices near the beginning of the year to catch the back-to-school market.

Thesauri

No writer can afford to be without a thesaurus of some kind. The standard *Roget's Thesaurus* appears in a number of different formats, at widely varying prices and under a number of publishers' imprints. Oxford, Chambers and Collins are always a safe bet. The *NZ Mini Thesaurus,* published by Bardsley, contains New Zealand-specific references. You may prefer to work with a subject-listed rather than an alphabetical thesaurus; if so, you could consider Penguin's revised editions. As with dictionaries, bookselling chains will often offer the most competitive prices.

Dictionaries of quotations

Something has been said about everything at some time, and most gems are recorded in dictionaries of quotations. Again, the range is large, the quality varies, and the basic rule of getting what you pay for applies. Quotations may be ordered alphabetically, by name, by date or by subject — choose the format with which you feel most comfortable. Every good dictionary of quotations should, however, have an index of keywords. The *Heinemann Dictionary of New Zealand Quotations* is a particularly rich source of indigenous pearls of wisdom, as is *Quotable New Zealanders* (Orsman, H. and Hurley, D. Auckland: Reed, 1992), a compendium of memorable remarks and reflections.

Other books

Writers will often find occasion to consult other reference books, but decisions about actually digging into your wallet need to be made on a case-by-case basis. Useful books include:

- atlases
- dictionaries of biography, in particular the five-volume *Dictionary of New Zealand Biography*
- specialist technical dictionaries and reference works in areas such as medicine, science, literature, geography and the arts
- business directories, such as those produced by Universal Business Directories and Wise
- New Zealand and Pacific Islands Yearbooks, available online
- *Who's Who*
- the *New Zealand Business Who's Who*
- encyclopedias, such as the *Bateman New Zealand Encyclopedia, New Zealand's Heritage* and *New Zealand's Nature Heritage;*
- dictionaries of dates and anniversaries, such as *Essential Dates: A Timeline of New Zealand History* by A. Dench (Auckland: Random House NZ, 2005), and the *Historical Dictionary of New Zealand* by K. Jackson and A. McRobie (Auckland: Longman, 1996)
- *Private Box and Bag Directory,* from New Zealand Post.

Revised editions of the *Style Book: A Guide for New Zealand Writers and Editors* (Wellington: GP Publications: 1995) may be purchased in most bigger bookshops, or consulted through libraries — it's a good general guide to New Zealand writing rules and styles.

Major libraries may hold one or more of the following media research publications, which are helpful to freelance writers:

PRRADS (Press Research Rate and Data System), compiled by Nielsen Marketing Research, Auckland. Volumes on television, radio and newspapers, and magazines, updated as information changes. Aimed primarily at advertisers, these directories are nevertheless a useful research source for writers investigating markets for their writing.

Nielsen Media Directory, published biannually by Nielsen Marketing Research, Auckland. A condensed version of the information contained in PRRADS, in one volume.

Press, Radio and TV Guide: Australia, New Zealand and Pacific Islands, published annually by Country Press, Australia. Contains brief details about newspapers, magazines, journals, radio and television in the South Pacific; aimed mainly at advertisers.

Personal computers (PCs)

The days of laboriously writing a manuscript by hand are long gone. Quite simply, no editor will consider a handwritten manuscript, so a computer with a word processing program (such as Microsoft Word) is essential if you wish to produce presentable work. Many editors and publishers accept submissions sent as email attachments. See Chapter 2 for a more detailed look at how you can utilise technology.

Work diary

Get into the habit of keeping a record of your activities for each piece of writing you do. A record of time spent on a project, of when and where you submitted it for publication and of the responses you get can be invaluable. Often a response from a busy editor or overseas publisher will be slow, and it is useful for you to build up your own picture of reasonable time-scales for reply. For the disorganised writer, such a diary can also avoid embarrassing duplication of work and correspondence, and it can provide an indication as to whether or not the time spent on writing is really worth the financial rewards received. If you regularly submit material to a number of publishers, perhaps a chart to display the progress of submissions from one publisher to the next would be useful. It might also help you prioritise those publishers who accept more than others.

A work diary should also include detailed accounts of expenditure and revenue. It should be of interest to all writers to know how much it is actually costing them to produce material. When keeping accounts, be sure to include all of the following:

- stationery
- photocopying
- photographic expenses
- books purchased
- magazines and newspapers purchased or subscribed to
- services, such as fax bureaus, Internet connections, typing services
- repairs to equipment, such as printers, or service contracts for personal computers
- permission fees, if you use copyright material in your own writing
- telephone charges relating to your writing
- postage and courier charges
- other costs, such as paying an accountant, attending a course, paying membership fees to writing organisations, etc.

Clippings file

Many magazines will provide you with a complimentary copy or two of the issue in which your work appears; newspapers are not always so good. Regardless of whether you have to buy a copy or not, you should always be certain to collect a sample of every piece of writing you have published. A range of sturdy folders with clear PVC envelope pages is available from stationers; also suitable for use as clippings files are photograph albums with self-sealing pages. Quite apart from keeping all your published work in good condition for your own satisfaction and future reference, a clippings file can be shown to prospective editors and employers if they express interest in commissioning work from you. Several of the journalism courses outlined in a later chapter also require a selection of clippings as a prerequisite for entry.

Albums and envelope folders have an advantage over other filing methods in that you can easily view and extract particular clippings to photocopy when necessary. Larger sizes are best — you won't have to cut and paste your writing to fit all on one page.

Once you have collected more than one folder's worth of clippings, slip a brief contents page inside the front cover of each album or folder, with dates and publication details for each item. This makes for easy reference when searching for a particular article.

Those who have a book or two to their name will also know how friends, acquaintances and neighbours always seem to want a free copy when they drop around. Always keep at least one copy in an 'archive'. Never give it away. Although you may be able to buy extra copies at a discount from the publisher, this is an added expense — and, with any luck, the publisher will one day run out of copies too. This means they won't be able to replace your valued first edition!

Notebook

Scraps of paper with brilliant midnight ideas scribbled on them are often difficult to find in the grey light of morning. An 'ideas' notebook, small enough to carry around, is a better idea. Write down anything that occurs to you and which you think has potential. Even if you cannot follow up on such ideas immediately, a notebook may prove fruitful when inspiration wanes. Small tape recorders can also be useful in interview situations.

Address book

Keep a separate address book containing the names, addresses and telephone numbers of every person, organisation or business contact you have used in your writing. Also include useful addresses and telephone numbers, such as the nearest photocopying service, a reputable local courier firm, photographic processors, secretarial services and the local library. Make sure you have an address book set up on your PC to record email addresses of all correspondents.

Stationery

Nothing can be more infuriating than completing a manuscript and finding you have run out of paperclips to hold it together, envelopes in which to post it, Fastpost stickers to ensure a speedy delivery or stamps to stick on your SAE. Always have plenty of materials on hand — buying in quantity saves time, frustration and money.

A ream (500 sheets) of white, bond A4 paper is best stored flat and in a dry place. Keep a number of ordinary manila, letter-size envelopes for use as SAEs. Also have white letter-size envelopes for smaller submissions and a good supply of white A4-size envelopes for larger projects.

If you work on a PC, keep a box of blank CDs on hand to regularly back up finished material or ongoing work which you may have stored on your PC. If your submission is lengthy, it will be easier and more cost effective to burn the material on to a CD, rather than printing it. It will also save considerably on postage costs.

Always keep a supply of ink cartridges for your printer – it is extremely frustrating to find out that you have run out of ink in the middle of printing out a submission.

Ensure you have ample supplies of all the following: paperclips, staples, pencils, erasers, Fastpost stickers, stamps for each envelope size, waterproof markers for addressing parcels and a clean sponge if you have lots of submissions to send and don't want to end up with a well-gummed tongue. A calculator will often come in handy. And you may like to consider getting a number of pre-printed labels with your name and address on them for a variety of uses.

New Zealand Post periodically puts out brochures about postal charges and the services it provides — you can save yourself a lot of queuing if you know what your letters and parcels are going to cost. The Business Post brochure, available from all New Zealand Post outlets, details such things as charges for standard and non-standard letters, bulk mail discounts, business reply post, freepost, international express services, proof of delivery and private boxes.

Buy stamps in bulk, as they are always valuable to have around. You should also find out the collection times for mail at your local post office or New Zealand Post agency. You can then set your own daily deadlines around these times.

Literary agents

In western countries up to three-quarters of mainstream books are handled by literary agents, who act as business managers for their author/clients.

New Zealanders, who have less acquaintance with the work of agents than, for example, New Yorkers, may well decide that the agent's commission is better saved, and that do-it-yourself is the way to go. However, literary agents can be very effective in managing the business side of an author's affairs, as well as employing a current and extensive knowledge of the book market and its publishers, and the film/television market and its producers. See Chapter 18 for a listing of literary agents and publishing consultants.

The commercial aspects of authorship — making a convincing submission to the best publishers or film producers, getting the best contract terms, and ensuring regular and full royalty payments — are complex activities. A skilled agent, who should have experience as a publisher, book editor and/or published writer, understands these complexities.

It is the agent's responsibility to make more money for you from your manuscripts than you could achieve yourself, and to be 'a true author's friend' and go-between through all the ups and downs of having a book published or a film made.

The agent works on a commission basis and, for this reason, must be selective as to which writers can be accepted as agency clients. Manuscripts that are likely to be published, in the agent's judgement, may well qualify their authors as new clients. Previously unpublished authors may find it as difficult to sign up with an agent as it is with a publisher. Usually a letter of enquiry should first be sent to the agent, listing qualifications, published works and aspirations, and enclosing a synopsis of the manuscript to be submitted. Perhaps six to eight double-spaced pages would comprise a typical submission.

Agents with publishing experience can provide useful advice in developing a book from a proposal or a manuscript, and in developing an on-going career in authorship. They are independent in judgement and should have an intimate knowledge of the structure and personalities of every publishing house, and thus which companies are best suited both to evaluating particular manuscripts and to marketing the resultant books at home and abroad.

Directories such as the UK produced *Writers' and Artists' Yearbook* (published annually by A & C Black) and the *Literary Market Place* (published annually for the US by Bowker) show how diverse publishing and production houses are, and how difficult it can be for the writer to achieve success in publication and/or production. The most recent editions of these are usually available in the reference section of all main centre libraries, or can be ordered on the Internet from online bookstores such as Amazon. Agents can help make the author's marketing more effective, and achieve a better income from book and film proposals and manuscripts.

2 Technology

Even writers who prefer to produce their first drafts in longhand will acknowledge how the use of PCs (personal computers) has revolutionised the production and progress toward publication of manuscripts. A PC with a word-processing program allows you to compile, store and present professional-looking manuscripts, and to keep presenting them in top condition until they sell.

Perhaps the greatest advantage of a PC is flexibility. Your manuscript becomes a living thing — something you can rework to your heart's content. An accurate word count is available in seconds, and reams of paper become condensed into a single CD, saving valuable storage space in your home office. Individual documents can be copied, transferred to a CD, or sent as an email attachment to the recipient. And all the operations you find yourself performing as a freelance writer — for example, composing standard covering letters, title pages and invoices — can be repeated in a fraction of the time, using pre-saved templates.

What do you get when buying a PC?

Hardware and software

For those who may be new to the use of information technology, there are two basic parts to a computer system — the hardware and the software. The hardware is the machinery, which comprises the box of essential electronics that control your computer, a colour monitor (the screen), a keyboard and a mouse. Additional items of hardware may include a printer, modem, scanner, and additional back-up devices. The software consists of the main program, or operating system that gives the machine the instructions to make it work and controls how everything appears to you on the monitor, plus extra programs for specific tasks such as word processing, spreadsheet calculations and graphs, presentations, accounting, and desktop publishing. Microsoft Office (or Open Office, free from http://www.openoffice.org/), for example, is an integrated suite of programs that covers all the above needs plus more, and includes the word-processing program called Microsoft Word. Your new PC will come preconfigured with one of the latest versions of an operating system installed, and you then have the choice of which additional software to load. This is perhaps one of the most important considerations, as it is the software that you will use to perform the variety of tasks involved in writing.

When selecting a computer, the saying 'you get what you pay for' is completely true. Reputable appliance stores are able to offer 'standard packages' at prices at the lower end of the market, reflecting their volume sales and buying power. For the first-time buyer, there will be safety in selecting a packaged solution which usually comes with a warranty of some sort — and the shop staff won't baffle you with lots of computer jargon. However, the technical know-how of the shop staff may be limited and they may not be able to assist you in making a decision as to which package best suits your needs. On the other hand, if you're familiar with computers and are looking to upgrade your current system, a specialist computer reseller will be able to provide expert knowledge and put together a customised package of goodies for you. The final result is likely to cost substantially more than an off-the-shelf package, but it will be tailored to your individual needs. In either case, you need to have done your homework beforehand, and have a very clear idea of what you want to achieve with your new PC.

Be aware that computer hardware capabilities are constantly changing and that software is updated regularly. Prices for PC packages are also fairly fluid, and it's worth checking to see if the extra special package on offer for a keen price is not a system which is about to be superseded by a new model, or version. The capabilities of PCs are being expanded all the time so the following information is intended as a general buyer guide only. Before you make a decision on a new PC check what's on offer from a range of outlets first to ensure you are getting a system that not only is good value but also has the most up-to-date specifications.

One of the things the salesman will want to discuss is how much 'memory' you want your computer to have. Memory describes how much work the computer can cope with at one time, and is measured in Mb, or megabytes. One Mb is equal to 1 million bytes (basically, one million characters, such as letters, spaces, and paragraph breaks). Your computer needs lots of memory for the operating system and for the additional software that you will install and memory is particularly important if you are handling large complex files, or are regularly downloading information from the Internet. Computers in the lower range will be around 512 Mb and systems that offer more than 1000 Mb are not unusual, with some packages offering 2048 Mb. More is definitely better and you should buy as much as you can afford, particularly if you are going to install something like Microsoft Office, which is very memory-hungry. Too little memory will mean that your computer runs sluggishly, and the programs won't function at the speed you require.

The brain of the computer is its processor, or CPU (central processing unit). These come in a number of types and are rated by the speed with which they process data, referred to as Megahertz (MHz; a measure of how many operations per second the CPU can perform). Generally, the faster the processing speed, the more powerful and, of course, the more expensive the computer will be. In reality, word processing applications will perform satisfactorily at the lower processor speeds.

The other area of memory to discuss is the hard drive, which is a very large internal storage area where all your data is held. With advances in microchip technology, it is now possible to buy a powerful computer with over 200 gigabytes (GB) of hard drive storage (one gigabyte = 1 billion bytes, or around 150 million words). Less expensive packages are around the 80 GB range, which will be more than enough for the average user.

Advances in the amount of memory (storage) being offered have been significant in the past few years and this upgrading process will most likely continue, especially now that PCs are being used to download material such as television programmes, videos and CDs.

One major choice that buyers do need to make before purchasing a computer is between the two main systems available in the personal computer market: the Windows PC system and the Macintosh system. The system you choose will depend on personal preference, of course, and also on what your colleagues and acquaintances advise. Both systems operate Microsoft Windows software packages and both systems provide an excellent end result. Macintosh systems, or 'Macs', tend to be used more by designers, as they have very accurate graphics applications, but PCs can do the job too. If you regularly supply one or two clients with written material, find out what system they use — it might save a little time and effort on everyone's part. Information can be swapped between systems, and compatibility problems which once used to be quite common are now rare. Specialist Mac distributors offer a variety of options if this is the system you decide to buy. As long as you are using the latest software, you are unlikely to encounter any compatibility problems.

Monitors, keyboards and choice of mouse

The monitor (formerly known as a VDU, or visual display unit) is the screen on which you can watch your masterpiece take shape. The standard size was 15 inches, but 17 inches is very common, and many PCs offer 19-inch and 21-inch screens. A bigger monitor reduces eye strain. particularly if you opt for a flat-screen LCD monitor, which takes up substantially less room on your desktop. Macintosh offer flat-screen systems that house all the boxed components too, which even further reduces the space needed for equipment.

Keyboards tend to be fairly standard — comfortable, durable, and energy-efficient. Also available is a so-called 'natural' keyboard: this is a keyboard that 'wraps round' the natural position of your fingers for ease of use.

Most machines also use a mouse to move the cursor around the screen. A mouse can be difficult to use at first, but people get used to them very quickly. There are a wide variety of types available, ranging from the standard two-button mouse through to those with special features such as scrolling third and fourth buttons, trackballs, and also wireless mice that use radio digital technology as well as those using infra-red transmission

Printers

The prices of both laser and inkjet printers have come down considerably in recent years, making them affordable to the home office user, and your choice of printer will be determined by your budget. Both types produce perfect copies and the growth in use of digital cameras has resulted in a corresponding rise in the quality of colour reproduction that the average printer offers.

Inkjet printers 'spit' ink onto the paper. They are capable of very high resolution (the number of dots, known as pixels, that go towards making up the image), and are very affordable — with some available for under $100. The more expensive versions, costing (at the time of writing) upwards of $250, offer outstanding quality colour reproduction. Their downside is slow speed and high running costs. Since for the average writer most printing will be in black, it is important, if selecting a colour printer, to choose one that has a black ink cartridge separate from the colour cartridge/cartridges.

Many printers are increasingly becoming multi-function pieces of equipment, combining features such as scanners, printers and digital copiers in one flatbed design.

If you absolutely must create the perfectly presented manuscript, but can't afford the higher quality printers, simply take your disk to a printer who will print it out for you easily and cheaply, as long as the software they use is compatible with the software you've used to create your document.

Scanners

A scanner is a piece of machinery rather like a photocopier that converts an image into a digitised computer file. They usually include the software which allows you to scan an image from, say, a photograph, drawing, or another book, and integrate this image with other documents. Scanners are rated according to the resolution they can achieve, usually rated in DPI (dots per inch). A good-quality scanner will include Optical Character Recognition (OCR) software which will 'read' images from scanned documents and extract the text from the picture. The text can then be readily edited and saved as a standard document. As mentioned, scanners are increasingly becoming integrated into new printer models.

Modems and routers

From the term modulator-demodulator, this is the piece of electronic wizardry that brings the Internet to your computer via your phone line.

It works by converting digital data into signals that can be transmitted over standard telecommunication lines, and vice versa.

PC packages sometimes come with an internal dial-up modem (one that is pre-installed inside the computer). A dial-up modem connects to the Internet service provider via the telephone wires, so the telephone cannot be used while you are on the Internet. Internet connections using DSL technologies, commonly called 'broadband', are a popular option. The advantages are speed and that the telephone can be used at the same time as the computer accesses the Internet.

Notebooks vs desktops

A desktop computer is one that generally features a large, heavy 'box' of electronics along with a separate keyboard and monitor that sit on top of your desk in your home office. The processor does not like to be moved around whilst the computer is operating (this can damage the hard drive). The advantages of a desktop computer are that the equipment tends to be bigger (larger, clearer keyboard; bigger monitor so less eye strain), and it is easier and cheaper to upgrade the component parts, such as the CD drive.

A notebook computer, on the other hand (the next evolutionary step up from a laptop), is about the size of a large folder. The 'base' comprises the processor, the keyboard and some sort of device for moving the cursor, and a hinged lid incorporates the monitor. It is generally more robust and a good deal lighter in weight. It offers the writer the great advantage of portability. You can take your work with you wherever you go — from one office to another, across town or across the world. Some versions offer screens as large as 17 inches. The big disadvantage of a notebook is its greater cost. They tend to become obsolete more quickly too, as it is more difficult to upgrade component parts. Notebooks are definitely sexier than desktops, but unless you absolutely have to be mobile to work efficiently, it may be hard to justify the extra cost.

You will need to back-up your work on a regular basis on both a desktop and a notebook, but more so on a notebook because if it is lost or stolen, so is your work! Back-up options used to be more limited for notebooks, but most will include CD/DVD writers (burners) as standard.

Both desktops and notebooks can be loaded up with powerful software, and both can access the Internet and transmit email.

Storing material

The work you do during a session is saved onto the hard drive, and should also be transferred or copied onto CDs or removable drives (flash drives) and stored away from your machine — a must if you want to keep your information secure.

The most common back-up device is currently the CD/DVD burner, a standard integrated component in modern computer systems. CD discs are inexpensive and it's worth keeping a good supply of them handy. You can use them for making copies to send to publishers and for archiving old material. Most importantly, you can make back-up copies of all your work, and keep them in a separate place AWAY from the computer. Learn how to use the back-up function of your PC, and get into the habit of making regular back-ups of your folders and files. Like all machines, computers sometimes suffer from malfunctions, or power surges, and the prevalence of Internet viruses (see Internet section in this chapter) which can indiscriminately gobble up files means that regular back-up and storing copies of work electronically is essential.

Getting the most from your software

The complexity of modern software means that most novice writers will never use the full potential of a word-processing program. The salesperson will only be able to provide a brief overview, and then it will be up to you to learn how to 'drive' your new machine. A program such as Microsoft Word allows you to:

- edit text (i.e., shift it, cut and paste it, delete or insert sections into it)
- type continuously without having to insert line breaks
- lay out pages and change the way they will appear on paper
- number and order pages
- see what a page will look like before it is printed out
- search for and replace individual words
- check your spelling, customise a dictionary, and look for other options from a thesaurus
- auto-correct any common mistakes, such as an incorrectly spelt word
- remove double spaces
- add comments or track changes that you may make to a document, which you can review at a later stage of the editing process
- choose from a number of typefaces, font sizes and styles to work with, and see how these look on screen
- undo your mistakes, and redo any changes
- count the number of words in a document automatically.

Fortunately, there is a proliferation of books covering all levels of computing, from complete beginners to those who want to learn how to write their own programs, and most community education centres and other centres of learning offer courses run by trained, qualified tutors. Check your local library's database for the training manual that matches the version of your program or visit a bookseller with a good computer book section.

Going online — the Internet and email

You can write your bestselling novel without access to the Internet, but you will be doing yourself a great disservice by missing out on a world of information. The Internet includes a number of services, of which the two most widely used are email and the World Wide Web (or, more simply, the 'web') — the latter, along with news groups, is discussed in more detail in Chapter 3. Most PC packages are supplied 'Internet ready', meaning that they have a modem and a web browser program, such as Microsoft Internet Explorer or Netscape Navigator, preinstalled. All you have to do is choose an Internet Service Provider (ISP), such as Xtra, Ihug, or Clear Net, and decide what subscription deal you want. The deal you choose will depend on how many hours you estimate you'll be online each month, and hence the dollar amount you're willing to pay. Broadband connections are increasingly becoming the rule. They offer a continual connection (no wasted time dialling up), superior speeds of access and downloading and do not tie up the phone line. Once you've signed up, the ISP will provide an installation disk for you to run on your computer or will talk you through the set-up process via their telephone helpline. Connect your modem to the phone line, and you're up and running. Your ISP will continue to provide free support via their helpline on an as-and-when-needed basis.

Email

Email (derived from 'electronic mail') has superseded the fax as a means of electronically transmitting a document across town, across country, or across the world and is infinitely cheaper than either post or courier, and is the fastest way of delivering your material. The software program is essentially a notepad in which you create, send and file messages either for storage in the 'outbox' or instant transmission.

The great advantages of email are that it is cheap, quick, and unobtrusive. And of course you can send multiple messages instantaneously to as many recipients as you like. Email messages are, by nature, short and to the point. When writing an email message to someone, think of it more as a memo rather than a letter — there's no need for time-consuming niceties, simply get straight to the point.

A document that contains anything other than straightforward text (such as complex formatting, graphics, or photographs), it is best sent as an 'attachment' Most email programs display an icon on the toolbar resembling a paperclip which, when selected, will allow you to attach to your message any file that you have stored on your computer. This file can be anything from a 300-page novel to a digital photograph, or a clip of video or recorded music. Although attachments take longer to send than plain-text emails, they still work out cheaper than post or courier, and are more reliable — you'll get a message from your ISP almost immediately if the message can't be sent for any reason (usually because you've typed the address incorrectly).

Email is an essential tool for most professional writers. Authors can submit manuscripts direct to the publisher along with attached photographs and illustrations (make sure you've made arrangements with them beforehand though — most publishers will not accept unsolicited manuscripts and attachments by email). These can then be emailed to an editor, who works directly on the text, cutting, pasting and shuffling material, and choosing and inserting the illustrations. Any correspondence between the editor and the author can be carried out by email, no matter what the geographical distance is between them. Once satisfied, the editor can email the finished manuscript back to the publisher who can them email it on to a typesetter. Journalists, too, depend on email for getting news copy and photographs to their editors to meet print deadlines.

However, there are a number of disadvantages with email, the most worrying being the potential to import computer viruses. A computer virus is, simply, a program designed to attach itself to another computer program. Some viruses damage the data on your disks by corrupting programs, deleting files, or even reformatting your entire hard drive. Most viruses, however, are not designed to do any serious damage; they simply replicate themselves or display messages. Viruses work by infecting executable program files, such as word processing, spreadsheet, or operating system programs. They do not damage hardware, such as keyboards or monitors.

Computer viruses are readily transmitted as attachments with what may appear to be benign email (e.g., an email addressed to you with the message 'For Your Information'). Once the attachment is opened, the virus is transmitted to your computer. To avoid becoming infected, be very wary of attached files, even those sent by your closest friends and professional organisations (some viruses replicate themselves by tapping into the email software's address book, and sending themselves to everyone listed therein!) and never open an attachment unless you are certain of its source. Install a good, up-to-date anti-virus program, as recommended by your ISP or computer support people, and set it to run continuously in the background. Keep it efficient by regularly downloading upgrades from the software provider.

Although the uses of the Internet are changing all the time, there are plenty of books to help keep you informed about the ever-changing technology. Try a bookseller who has a good selection of computer books, or peruse your library's database. Easy to read and understand examples include *The Complete Idiot's Guide to the Internet and Windows XP* (published by Que), *The Rough Guide to the Internet* (published by Rough Guides), and *The Internet for Dummies* (published by IDG Books). Make sure you use a book that is no more than a year old.

3 Research in New Zealand

Research is an integral part of the craft and process of writing — both fiction and non-fiction. Credibility is the key to success, and the first step to gaining it is getting your facts right. No matter what form your writing takes, research will be a constant part of your routine, and it is essential that you familiarise yourself with the sources of information available to you.

It is important that you have a clear idea of the purpose and scope of your writing before beginning any research, and in the case of longer pieces, it is essential to plan both the research and the writing together. Being aware of the precise nature of your article or book will enable you to write down, first, what you need to know, and second, where you can find that information. When you work to a deadline, allow enough time for research — a short piece may require only a few telephone calls, but a detailed story or book may require many hours of painstaking research. Be aware of the time you are spending — and be ready to build that into the cost of the finished product if you have been commissioned, or are working at an hourly rate.

The Internet and the World Wide Web

The Internet is an invaluable research tool (see Chapter 2 for what you need to get connected). If offers easy and rapid results to any researcher seeking information on just about anything anywhere in the world. What might have taken hours to find in a library a few years ago (and then would probably have been out of date) is immediately accessed from your own desktop simply by clicking your mouse a few times. The answer to a query is often just an email away.

The most important part of the Internet is the 'World Wide Web', most usually referred to simply as 'the web', which is an infinite collection of linked pages of information covering every subject imaginable. To read these pages you need a browser, such as Microsoft's Internet Explorer (usually supplied free on your ISP's installation disk or often 'bundled' with other software programs). Each page on the web has its own unique address, usually beginning with http://www (e.g., Telecom's online version of its White Pages can be found at www.whitepages.co.nz). Any page anywhere in the world can be downloaded, just about immediately, at the cost of whatever subscription package you have signed up for with your ISP. Frequently the web page will include 'hyperlinks' (think of them as jumping-off points) to other related pages or other websites, which provide an elaborate and extensive cross-referencing system.

The web's 'index' lies in the many 'search engines' that are available to web users. Type in a key word or phrase, and the search engine will list all the sites it can find that contain that word or phrase, along with links to other sites. Beware — heading off down a particular line of research, following links through a number of different sites, can be time-consuming and completely engrossing. The most commonly used search engine is presently www.google.co.nz

One of the wonderful features of the Internet is that there is no one regulatory organisation, and absolutely anyone anywhere can set up a website. However, this means that so-called 'facts' published on an organisation's 'official' website may in fact be complete fiction. Other sites — such as www.wikipedia.org — appear to be bona fide encyclopedias to the uninitiated but information can be altered by anyone who visits the site.

Beware of getting your facts right. Always check the source of the information, and that the website is published by a reputable company or organisation. Look for an actual address and contact phone and fax numbers to check the legitimacy of the company publishing the information. Most of New Zealand's larger organisations, associations and societies have their own website, and many list their press releases within these pages. Checking these on a regular basis and keeping copies of newsworthy articles can be of great assistance when compiling facts for an article or feature.

Another useful source of information is the incredible number of discussion groups and news groups, where individuals can sign in and 'chat' online to other group members. Their quality varies considerably, and some can be very cliquey, but a well-timed question can often elicit information that you desperately need. The best strategy is to join one or two appropriate groups that interest you, listen in for a while to read other members' messages and to get the tone and style of the group, then have a go at 'posting' your own message or question. Beginners can avoid making the usual learner blunders by reading the group's FAQ — an information sheet containing 'frequently asked questions', and an item that is a goldmine of information in its own right.

Written resources

New Zealand is fortunate in having a wealth of written resources available, some dating back to the nation's earliest days. There are books on most New Zealand topics, and these are an invaluable source of information. While you should have your own collection of essential reference books, every library will be able to provide you with ample opportunity for research into most topics — time devoted to learning how to use their catalogue, computer database, online resources, and microfiche readers is time well spent, and for difficult or obscure enquiries, your librarian is your most important resource. New Zealand Books in Print (D.W. Thorpe, Auckland, published annually) is an invaluable, regularly updated reference for New Zealand books — all libraries should have a copy, complete with the regular updates that are published each year.

Most major libraries now have websites which have a listing of their complete catalogue, which can be searched by author, title, subject, key words, etc. This can prove invaluable when looking for a specific book title or relevant material. Title searches will indicate which libraries in a specific region stock the title, and whether or not it is available on loan. Public libraries throughout New Zealand can be accessed through the website www.nzlibraries.com which provides relevant links to library sites.

When collecting information from books, it is important to note all the relevant details about the book itself, even if you do not intend to refer to it directly in your writing. Such records can be useful to you in future research, and can save time if you do decide to construct a bibliography. When you pick up a book, check the date of publication first — some books become obsolete quickly; then skim-read the first chapter to get an idea of the author's style and viewpoint. Never treat one book as the authoritative work, even if it is acclaimed as such; try to read as widely as possible on your chosen topic to get a balanced view. Record the addresses of any websites that have provided useful information by creating 'Favourites' folders sorted by subject, but remember that addresses often change over a period of time. The same discipline applies when using the Internet to download information.

If you are writing for newspapers or magazines, make an effort to hunt down articles that have been previously published in the area you are researching. Most libraries will hold some form of periodicals abstract, usually published annually, updated on microfiche or accessed online, and they will often have a clippings file or index to articles in the periodicals to which they subscribe themselves. Ask about Index New Zealand (INNZ) — this contains abstracts of selected New Zealand serial publications, including newspapers and nearly 300 New Zealand journals about New Zealand and the South Pacific. Comprehensive coverage of titles extends from 1987 onwards and approximately 2,000 documents are added monthly. Subjects covered include general interest material, social research, current affairs, the arts and humanities. National Library's Reference and Alexander Turnbull Library staff have also retrospectively indexed many New Zealand titles. To find out more about accessing Index New Zealand online, visit the site www.natlib.govt.nz or email tepuna@natlib.govt.nz or phone 0508 837 862. For more information about content or editorial policy, contact the National Library's Indexing Services, email indexnz@natlib.govt.nz. Alternatively, photocopies of all items can be requested from the National Library, P.O. Box 1467, Wellington, email information@natlib.govt.nz.

Try to follow up as many sources as you can, by reading carefully any bibliographies listed at the rear of books or the end of articles, and tracking down further references as needed.

Encyclopedias can be useful as sources of general background information, as are directories of business organisations and government departments, *Who's Who*, specialist dictionaries, digests of statistics, yearbooks and other reference books. Every library will have a respectable reference section where these may be consulted — if in doubt, ask your librarian. He or she may be able to conduct a computer search of the New Zealand Bibliographic Network to ascertain whence and how other related publications may be borrowed for you.

Larger libraries will hold publications intended for a smaller, more specific audience, such as government or corporate literature (reports, discussion documents, etc.), publications by special interest groups, and other material of local or community interest.

Major government departments and businesses will often operate their own library and press clipping services in their specialist area, and these sources can be invaluable. An approach to either the Librarian or Public Relations Officer is the best way to make first contact and to see if these facilities are available for use by the general public. It is always best to try to do your research in person, as it may take a long time to get a response to written enquiries; even then, you cannot be sure the respondent will be as clear about your needs as you are.

Specialist libraries in New Zealand

A list of public libraries can be found in Public Libraries of New Zealand, published annually by the New Zealand Library Association. Other specialist collections, business libraries, etc., are noted in several publications available at most major libraries.

National Library of New Zealand — Te Puna Matauranga o Aotearoa

The National Library holds rich and varied collections of research material, primarily about New Zealand. It also houses the Alexander Turnbull Library which specialises in documentary materials — books, manuscripts, photographs, drawings and prints, music, newspapers, maps and oral history tapes — relating to New Zealand and the Pacific. Items from the National Library collections can be interloaned through a public or tertiary library or accessed by visiting the Library. Material from the Alexander Turnbull Library collections can only be used onsite, although copies can be made of most material (subject to copyright restrictions). The Library's online collections, catalogues and directories can be accessed free of charge at www.natlib.govt.nz.

A reference service is also available, which can be contacted via email at reference@natlib.govt.nz, or by post at P.O. Box 1467, Wellington; phone (04) 474 3030 or fax (04) 474 3070. While reference staff can assist with most requests, it is normally not possible for them to undertake ongoing in-depth research on behalf of clients. For any queries about how the system works, contact information@natlib.govt.nz or phone (04) 474 3000 or fax (04) 474 3035.

The library is located on the corner of Molesworth and Aitken Streets in Wellington, and is open from 9.00 am to 5.00 pm Monday to Friday, and 9.00 am to 1.00 pm Saturday.

University and College of Education libraries

University libraries often hold specialised collections of academic material relevant to the courses they offer. They also hold copies of research done by members of their staff, and theses written by their students. Colleges of education may also hold valuable references for work in education and, particularly, children's writing and publishing. You will generally have to visit these libraries in person if you wish to use their collections, but a preliminary letter of enquiry to ascertain if they will be of use to you may well be a good idea. Most academic libraries now have comprehensive websites which offer many options for searching their catalogues, and email addresses or direct Internet links to relevant members of staff who can help you with enquiries. The addresses of New Zealand universities and colleges of education are given below; in each case, postal correspondence should be addressed to The Librarian, University (or College) Library.

Auckland University of Technology, Private Bag 92006, Auckland 1142.
Tel (09) 921 9999 Website www.aut.ac.nz/library

Christchurch College of Education, P.O. Box 31065, Ilam. Christchurch 8030.
Tel (03) 348 2059 Fax (03) 348 4311 Website www.cce.ac.nz

Dunedin College of Education, Private Bag 1912, Dunedin.
Tel (03) 477 2289 Fax (03) 477 6573 Website www.dce.ac.nz

Faculty of Education, University of Auckland, Private Bag 92602, Symonds Street, Auckland 1035.
Tel (09) 623 8899 Fax (09) 623 8898 Website www.education.auckland.ac.nz

Lincoln University, P.O. Box 84, Lincoln 7647, Canterbury.
Tel (03) 325 2811 Fax (03) 325 2944. Email info@lincoln.ac.nz

Massey University, Private Bag 11054, Palmerston North.
Tel (06) 356 9099 Fax (06) 350 5645 Email asklib@massey.co.nz

University of Auckland, Private Bag 92019, Auckland 1020.
Tel (09) 373 7599 Website www.library.auckland.ac.nz

University of Canterbury, Private Bag 4800, Christchurch.
Tel (03) 364 2987x 8723 Fax (03) 364 2055 Email library@canterbury.ac.nz

University of Otago, P.O. Box 56, Dunedin.
Tel (03) 479 8910 Fax (03) 479 8947 Website www.library.otago.ac.nz

University of Waikato, Private Bag 3105, Hamilton.
Tel (07) 838 4466 x 8169 Fax (07) 838 4899
Website www.waikato.ac.nz/library

Victoria University of Wellington, P.O. Box 3438, Wellington
Tel (04) 463 6186 Fax (04) 477 2070 Website www.vuw.ac.nz/library

During research, you will often find yourself copying passages from the various publications you consult. If you intend to use these passages as direct quotations in your writing, make sure they are accurately transcribed, and that a full note is made of the publication in which they appear — i.e., publisher, place of publication, date, page reference, full title, edition and author or editor.

If you wish to quote a fairly long passage — for instance 300 or more words of prose, a complete poem, or 40 or more lines from a long poem — you should ask permission of the publisher. Some authors and publishers will be happy to agree without making a charge, but others may not.

If you are putting together major articles or books, you may find it useful to set up a card system of references, using key words or concepts to organise the material you discover during research. See the Appendices of this book for notes on accurate bibliography notes.

Photographic collections

When doing preliminary research using previously published books, note down the sources of any relevant illustrations and photographs which they contain. You need not use the same pictures, but you may be able to get a clearer idea of where suitable illustrations can be obtained. It can take months to track down photographs or slides held in private collections — so why duplicate the work that somebody has already done? There are also several photographic libraries in New Zealand, with general or specific collections, and these are listed below.

Many photographic libraries, such as the Alexander Turnbull Library, have extensive digital collections which can be searched and downloaded online.

Terms and conditions for using photographs may be obtained by writing to individual libraries. In some cases, reproductions may be acquired free of charge — in other cases, fees start at about $20 for a print or transparency, depending on size.

Each collection will also have its own requirements regarding credit notification or courtesy notice on publication. In every case, you should inform the library on your initial approach of how you will be using the photograph or transparency.

Alexander Turnbull Library, P.O. Box 12349, Wellington.
www.natlib.govt.nz
Nineteenth and twentieth century New Zealand.

Auckland City Library, P.O. Box 4138, Auckland 1.
www.aucklandcitylibraries.com
Historical Auckland.

Carter Observatory, P.O. Box 2909, Wellington.
www.carterobs.ac.nz
Astronomy.

Christchurch City Libraries, P.O. Box 1466, Christchurch.
Email library.christchurch.org.nz
Christchurch and Canterbury history.
Gisborne Museum and Art Centre, P.O. Box 716, Gisborne 3815.
www.tairawhitimuseum.org.nz
Local history.
Hawke's Bay Museum, P.O. Box 248, Napier.
www.hawkesbaymuseum.co.nz
Regional history.
Museum of New Zealand, Te Papa Tongarewa, P.O. Box 467, Wellington.
www.tepapa.govt.nz
New Zealand, Maori and Pacific Islands history.
Nelson Provincial Museum, P.O. Box 853, Nelson.
Email enquiries@museumnp.org.nz
Provincial.
North Otago Museum, P.O. Box 50058, Oamaru 8920.
Email museum@waitaki.govt.nz
Provincial.
Otago Settlers Museum, P.O. Box 566, Dunedin 9015.
www.otago.settlers.museum
Provincial.
Palmerston North City Library, P.O. Box 1948, Palmerston North.
citylibrary.pncc.govt.nz
Manawatu subjects.
Rotorua Museum of Art and History, Private Bag, Rotorua.
www.rotoruamuseum.co.nz
Rotorua and volcanic plateau regions.
Waikato Museum of Art and History, Private Bag 3010, Hamilton.
www.waikatomuseum.org.nz
Local history and industry.
Walsh Memorial Library, Museum of Transport and Technology,
P.O. Box 44114, Point Chevalier, Auckland.
Technology.
Wanganui City Library, Private Bag 3005, Wanganui.
www.wanganuilibrary.com
History, Whanganui River.
Whanganui Regional Museum, P.O. Box 352, Wanganui 5015.
Maori, local, industry, history.
Wellington Maritime Museum, P.O. Box 893, Wellington.
www.nzmaritime.org.nz
Maritime.
Wellington City Library, P.O. Box 1992, Wellington.
www.wcl.govt.nz
Local subjects.

As with other research, relevant businesses, organisations and government departments may also be approached for illustrations. In most cases, if suitable photographs are held, they will be happy to oblige, in return for a copy of the eventual article or book.

In addition to these libraries, there are a number of commercial image libraries throughout the country that can be looked up in Telecom's Yellow Pages (use the online version if looking nationwide: www.yellowpages.co.nz) or searched for using engines such as Google. Photographs from these photo-libraries can be expensive (around $80–$200 per image or more, depending on use) but the material they hold is always of the best quality. It's probably unwise to actually pay for a lot of photographs if you haven't secured a contract from a publisher. Most publishers regularly use these libraries anyway, so they may prefer to select their own images if there is going to be considerable expense involved.

Focus New Zealand, P.O. Box 84153, Westgate, Auckland 0657.
Tel (09) 411 5416 Fax (09) 411 5417
www.focusnzphoto.co.nz
New Zealand images.

Getty Images, P.O. Box 5636, Wellesley St, Auckland.
Tel 0800 462 431
www.gettyimages.com
Sports, leisure, science and international subjects.

PhotoNewZealand PO Box 1112 Christchurch
Tel (03) 377 7161 Fax (03) 982 7001
www.photonewzealand.com

Research for fiction

Getting the facts correct is no less important in fiction than in non-fiction. Although fiction writing necessarily employs a degree of imagination, most works are nevertheless set within a given time-scale and place. Although human activities, emotions and thoughts may be invented and altered to create a character within a novel or short story, the environment in which the characters act out their roles may well be easily identified by the reader — and glaring mistakes can spoil the whole effect. Maps, street guides, gazettes and other publications will lend accuracy to geographic descriptions of places in other times and areas; contemporary photographic records, biographies, works of fiction and social histories will give enough detailed information about lifestyles in other places and times to help you transport the reader effortlessly to your intended setting.

Examine the genre you are writing for, and decide for yourself what facts you need to check and which you can leave up to your own creative talents. Aspects of life you may need to research could include technology, common forms of speech, acceptable behaviour in other societies or times, costume, types of employment, local geographic peculiarities, contemporary affairs relating to your characters' lives, social customs, religious customs and frames of reference (i.e., what your characters could reasonably be expected to know about their world).

Interviews

First-hand research will involve talking to people and, in some cases, setting up formal interviews. Useful interviews require a good deal of skill (and confidence) on the part of the interviewer, but they can often make the difference between a dull story and a lively one. Many New Zealand magazines and newspapers are interested in the colourful human angle and it is almost impossible to inject this into your writing if you don't physically go out and talk with your subject.

Preparation makes all the difference between a good and bad interview. Setting up the interview should be done by telephone, and you should make what you are aiming to do quite clear to the interviewee (e.g., you want to talk about his or her hobby for a national magazine article, and you'd also like to take some photographs). Background research is essential for establishing the questions that need to be asked, and to whom they should be addressed. A list of questions should be prepared well in advance, and each should have a specific point. An interview is not a battle of wits — it is a conversation, and will succeed much better if both people are set at ease straight away. If you are not sure what you want from the interview, and the other person is unsure why you are there, the whole procedure will be a failure. Don't waste your time and the other person's as well — be prepared.

Although some people feel uncomfortable about speaking while a tape recorder is running (sometimes for good reason), it can be an invaluable aid when conducting an interview. Always ask for permission to use one at the outset of the session — if it is refused, write answers in a notebook. If there are no objections, try to keep the tape recorder unobtrusive — it is you who are interviewing, not the machine. Ideally, the person to whom you are speaking should forget the tape recorder is even there. Battery-operated tape recorders are best (otherwise you'll have to search for a power point), and good, external microphones provide the best quality recording. Have plenty of tapes, and check the recording levels before you start. Always check that your equipment is working properly.

Whether transcribing or tape-recording an interview, never rely on your memory, and always be wary of other people's — at the end of the interview, check the facts thoroughly before submitting any article to an editor. It is often useful to note during the interview anything about the people you are talking with, which may be used as interesting 'colour' in your final article — the way they dress, sit, speak, ponder, etc. Are they uncomfortable? Self-assured? Charming? Unpleasant? What do their voices sound like? Their laughter? Often the way someone says something will be much more interesting than the words that are actually used. Remember, too, to note physical characteristics. Your readers will want a visual impression of these people, as well as an oral one. Are they slight? World-weary? Do they have a happy face? What is their hair like? Do they use their hands a lot while speaking? Is there anything else which sets them apart from others?

4 Presentation

Some writers go to extraordinary lengths to sell their work. One American enthusiast even had special typing paper made, each sheet bearing a large, watermarked YES, the theory being that editors thumbing through his manuscripts would have subliminal urges to think positively with each turn of the page. Of course, it could only happen in the United States; judgement is reserved as to whether or not this method would work in New Zealand.

Presentation is, however, of crucial importance in marketing anything, and manuscripts are no exception. A mechanically sound car which is battered, rusty and smeared with grease will be slow to sell; a dog-eared manuscript encrusted with correction fluid and daubed with inky fingerprints will face similar problems.

There are certain rules that should always be followed in submitting a manuscript:

- all text should be double-spaced
- text should be on one side only of white A4 paper
- black ink should normally be used
- bond paper, rather than thinner bank, should be used
- there should be at least 25 mm of margin on the left side and at the head and foot of each page to allow editorial or printer's instructions
- text should be unjustified, i.e., ragged-edged on the right
- each page should have the same number of lines on it
- quotations should be indented, italicised, in smaller point size or identified as such in some consistent manner
- titles of other publications should be indicated by underlining or italics in a consistent manner
- special typesetting instructions should be marked in the left-hand margin
- consistent styles with regard to bibliographic references should be used throughout, in line with the publisher's editorial policy
- pins or staples should not be used to hold a manuscript together — editors and printers prefer to work with loose pages
- all pages should be numbered consecutively

- the final page should bear the footnote 'copy ends'
- an accurate word count should be supplied
- one original and one clean copy of the manuscript should arrive together
- the whole manuscript should arrive on the editor's desk at one time — not in sections
- if you are submitting your work on computer disk, ensure your system and software are compatible with the publisher's system
- ensure all computer disks are clearly labelled with the title of the manuscript, author's name, contents (e.g., Chapters 1–7), and the program the disk is in (e.g., Word 2000)
- text on computer disk should have minimal formatting (e.g., style tags, font types, indenting) because the publisher will send it to a designer to lay out
- two paper copies should be supplied with a computer disk
- ALWAYS keep a copy of everything.

A word processor and a desktop laser printer do the best job, but a manual typewriter will provide perfectly adequate text, as long as all the letters appear cleanly and your typing pressure is even, otherwise your presentation may look unprofessional. Manuscripts produced from near-letter-quality dot matrix printers are also acceptable to most editors. Electric typewriters using daisy-wheels will also produce a high-quality finish to your manuscript. With any word processor, avoid using strange typefaces, such as 'joined-up writing'.

Assuming your manuscript is competently written and directed to a carefully chosen market (along with the dozen or so other pieces the editor has received that morning) what else can you do to enhance your chances of success?

The first thing an editor sees is your envelope, so start your marketing there. An A4 envelope will mean your manuscript arrives uncreased and looking as tidy as when you posted it, and a piece of thin card inserted into the envelope can help when a particularly special presentation is required. White envelopes cost a few cents more but can create a more favourable impression than manila envelopes. Your envelope should bear the publisher's full postal address, preferably typed or written in waterproof ink. A short phone call to the publishing companies you propose sending your manuscripts to will often uncover the names of the people you need to see your work (the features editor, news editor, managing editor, etc.) and that name can be added to the bottom left-hand corner, marked 'Attention'. All mail should have a return address clearly marked on the reverse.

A writer's next weapon is the covering letter. This is the one page of your submission on which you simply cannot afford to make a mistake. A covering letter should be brief, to the point and catch the reader's interest. You should include the title of your work, a sentence or two describing its content and relevance (i.e., why the editor should read it) and a word count to enable him or her to assess its likely size in final publication format. (For books, estimates correct to within 1000–5000 words are acceptable; for articles, word counts should be rounded to the nearest 50 words.) You may also like to mention any expertise or qualifications you have in the subject area.

A sensibly-sized envelope, stamped and addressed, should always be attached to the covering letter for the return of your manuscript. If you do not require its return, say so, but still include a SAE for notification of rejection or acceptance. If a publisher hasn't asked for your material and, after reading it, doesn't want to use it, why should they have to pay to return it to you? If a SAE is not enclosed, some publishers will simply dump the manuscript if they decide not to use it, so be warned.

Payment is a matter to be discussed and decided on in each case. Often an offer to accept a publisher's usual rates will suffice. Be business-like (unless you know an editor personally) and never attempt to sway them with personal or professional compliments. You should resist the temptation to have fancy letterheads on your notepaper, and all letters should end with a request for the publisher to contact you in the event of his or her being interested in using your material. A typical letter to a newspaper or magazine publisher might follow the form on the following page.

Once you have the editor's attention, he or she should turn over your letter and see your title page. This should have the title of your work in capitals, any subtitle in capitals and lower case, and the word count should appear once more. As some editors use the title page to send to their accounts department to authorise payment, your full name, address and telephone number should also be included.

When submitting a manuscript to a newspaper or magazine, it is sometimes helpful to duplicate the first word of the next page at the bottom right-hand corner (under the last line) to help the reader keep an even reading pace. The end of your text should be clearly marked as such so that the reader can be sure there is nothing missing. A 'copy ends' legend will suffice; a blank page or page bearing a short biographical note about yourself (where appropriate) will confirm this. All the pages of your manuscript should be numbered consecutively.

Text should be neat throughout; spelling should be correct, or, if there is some doubt, at least consistent. Check that your sentences are grammatically correct and that the style follows that of the target publication as closely as possible. Give your editor something which will require a minimum of work in order to be slotted into the next issue and your chances of success will be considerably enhanced.

The same procedure should be followed, more or less, for books. Treat each chapter as if it were a separate article, and attach to the beginning of each a title page, displaying the book title, the chapter title, the page numbers contained within and a word count for that chapter. It will do no harm for your name and address to appear on chapter title pages either. One way

14 Main Street
Nelson

The Editor,
Advanced Woodcraft,
P.O.Box 9000,
Dargaville

9 May 2007

Dear Sir/Madam,
I would be pleased if you would consider the enclosed manuscript, entitled 'A Hardwood Project', for publication in Advanced Woodcraft. This 600-word article deals with the particular problems of obtaining suitable hardwood imports in New Zealand, and contains several supply ideas which your readers might find useful.

Should you wish to discuss the article, I may be contacted at the above address, or telephoned during business hours. You are welcome to use 'A Hardwood Project' at your usual rates. If, however, you feel you cannot use it at this time, I would appreciate its return and have enclosed a SAE for this purpose.

Yours faithfully,

Charles Chisel
Member, NZ Wood Retailers' Federation.
Tel (09) 999 9999
Email: charleschisel@charles.chisel

of ordering the chapters and various other matter is outlined below; there are other ways, and often not all of the parts listed are needed. Look through other books put out by your publisher to see which style is preferred.

1. Title page
2. Dedication or quotation, if desired
3. Contents
4. Acknowledgments
5. Introduction or Foreword (often by someone other than the author)
6. Preface (by the author, to introduce the book)
7. A list of illustrations
8. The main body of the text, split into chapters
9. Appendices
10. Notes on the text, by chapter
11. Glossary
12. Bibliography
13. Index

Additional material for scripts

Scripts for radio, television or theatre should be accompanied by a brief outline of the story, a character list and a scene list. Producers often prefer a manuscript to be bound in some way — plastic mouldings which slip over the spine of a collection of pages bind firmly, but are easily removed for photocopying, if need be.

Commissioned work

Where you have been specifically commissioned to write an article, you should ensure that everything the editor wanted has been included. You should go through your contract and any other notes you may have made or received from the editor and check each item off to ensure that you are submitting a complete package. Editors who are forced to spend a lot of additional time cleaning up and revising commissioned work are unlikely to approach you again. You should always ensure that your submission will reach your editor by the agreed date.

Multiple submissions

Whether or not you wish to submit your manuscript to more than one publisher at a time is up to you, but given that the New Zealand market is as small as it is, it should not be difficult to target your most likely prospect. Multiple submissions are not recommended for newspapers or magazines, because of the short deadlines they use. Sometimes, they may use a story immediately it comes to hand, and inform you later. If you've sent the manuscript to a number of publications at the same time, this could have embarrassing results. Multiple submissions may, however, be of some worth to book authors, in terms of time spent waiting for different publishers to assess your work.

You must be very careful to keep track of what you have sent where; and as soon as a manuscript is accepted, you must write to the other prospective publishers withdrawing your offer of the manuscript. Publishers who may have spent considerable time looking over your work in the interim may not be pleased to have you withdraw it later. The risk is for you to assess.

If you are sending several stories under one covering letter, make sure that your name and address is on every single title page. Often, batches of manuscripts will get split up in the reading and selection process, and if the editor can't find out who wrote a particular piece, you, the author, haven't been doing your job properly!

Electronic submissions

Many companies are wary of accepting material that has been submitted by electronic means — be it as an email attachment or on a disk. With the infinite variety of viruses that can be transmitted via email (and spread through infected disks), many editors will not even open email attachments. A phone call beforehand to the editor will determine their policy on accepting electronic submissions.

Conclusion

The whole package that you present to an editor should be authoritative and stand out as the work of a professional. Remember that editors look over hundreds of submissions each year; any extra touches you can think of to make your work stand out will always be worthwhile. Remember, also, that the best marketing in the world won't shift a bad product. The real selling begins when the editor starts to read your draft.

A note on patience

In newspaper or magazine publishing, things may happen pretty quickly, especially if your market research has been done properly and you have prepared just the right article at the right time. In book publishing, however, patience truly is a virtue. Nothing will make an editor make up his or her mind quicker than having an author continually calling or writing to enquire about the status of their manuscript. (You may think that is exactly what you want, but be warned that the decision will often be in the negative to simply remove the source of irritation!) Book editors may often have a manuscript read by one or two other people; they will have to pass it by their marketing and sales force to gain their impressions; if they are linked up with overseas publishers, they may wish to send it overseas for comment on its suitability for foreign markets. If you've provided a 300-page manuscript, remember that it TAKES TIME!

Most publishers will acknowledge manuscripts received and will generally let you know how long an assessment will take. If you want to create a good relationship with your publisher, let him or her do their job in that time without interruption. If a considerable length of time passes without a word from them, then make polite enquiries. Most publishers will be only too happy to explain what their selection process involves, and where your manuscript is 'in the system', but trying to push for quick answers is not good business. The publisher needs to do their own market research, in an acceptable time frame, just as much as you do.

5 Photography and Illustrations

Photographs

If you are writing for a publication that regularly uses photographs as illustrations you may be able to supplement your writing income, and increase your chances of a sale at the same time, by providing the editor with photographs that he or she can use. Good photography is a skill that cannot be covered within the scope of this book; there are, however, numerous books and magazines available in New Zealand which are devoted to improving your technique behind the camera. What you can do with a camera is more important than the make or style of the camera itself, but most writers wishing to take photographs for their articles will find a 35 mm single-lens reflex camera more than adequate for their needs. If you do not feel confident using a camera, it may be worthwhile enrolling in a photography class — look through your local newspaper or community college brochures to find a course that will suit your needs.

By examining copies of your target publications you will see what sort of photographs are generally used in terms of subject, style and format. Some magazines require high-quality colour transparencies; most newspapers use black and white prints, although many papers have moved to occasional colour, particularly on front-page and feature stories. Whatever the requirements, the basics of good, saleable photographs remain the same. They must be well-composed and not cluttered with extraneous detail; they should be clear and in focus; they should have good contrast or accurate colour; they should be relevant; and they must form an integral part of the package you deliver to the editor.

Some newspapers and magazines like to have photographs submitted with articles, while others prefer to find their own illustrations. Community newspapers and smaller publications will nearly always prefer you to supply photographs. The directory section of this book will give you an indication of which publications prefer to have photographs submitted to them.

The most acceptable sizes for photographs are 35 mm for transparencies and 6′ x 8′ for black and white prints. Black and white photographs should be printed on glossy paper. Negatives are not usually acceptable, as prints are made directly into halftone plates. Square format, or 120-size, transparencies give a much higher quality in printing, but they require expensive cameras and are usually the realm of the professional photographer.

Where photographs are desirable, they should be submitted with the text of an article. Where this is not possible, but you are able to supply photographs, you should clearly state in your covering letter that photographs are available if the article is used. Conversely, you should not waste an editor's time by offering to provide photographs if you cannot do so. With rare or fragile photographs, copies or photocopies only should be sent with unsolicited articles.

Every photograph you submit should be adequately captioned. For prints, you may wish to type captions on a strip of paper which is then stuck to the rear of the photograph with adhesive tape, or you may prefer to use self-adhesive labels. Each print should also bear your name and address somewhere on the reverse. Where there could be possible confusion about the correct orientation of a photograph, the top should be clearly arrowed on the reverse and labelled as such. Transparencies mounted in cardboard or glass should not be submitted — each one must be in a separate transparency envelope or paper sheet, with the caption written upon it. A caption sheet should also be included with your covering letter, listing the captions for each photograph next to a brief outline of what is in the shot. With transparencies, a pencil sketch showing the main features in outline can be useful in ensuring that the transparency is reproduced the right way up, i.e., not back to front.

Writing effective captions is as much an art as the photography itself. Captions should always explain clearly and concisely what the picture is about. Who is in it? What is it of? How is it related to the text of your article? Try to tie the caption in with the article itself and examine the language used for captions in your target publication. Emulate its style and try to imagine how the photograph will appear in that particular publication.

It is not unusual for some book contracts to specify the number and scope of illustrations that an author is expected to supply at his or her own cost. This can be an advantage to the author, as he or she knows exactly what the book should contain. If you are providing photographs for a book, indicate in your manuscript roughly where you think the photographs should be placed within the text. Some publishers will require authors to furnish a photograph of themselves for reproduction on the back cover or dust jacket of their books — it is normally the responsibility of the author to pay for this photograph.

Photographs may be cropped or scaled to fit the requirements of a particular publication, or to remove unnecessary detail. It is usually best merely to indicate where you think a photograph should be cropped (if you must do it yourself, use a Chinagraph pencil available from all artists' suppliers). Scaling a photograph (working out how much it should be enlarged or reduced to fit a given space) should in most cases be left to the editor or designer. There are limits as to how much a print can be enlarged before the grain of the photograph becomes too noticeable, and it is usually better to leave these sorts of decisions to someone with an expert eye.

Photographs should always be sent in individual translucent photograph envelopes, available singly or in bulk from most photographic retailers. Always submit more photographs than you think will be necessary, so the editor or designer will have a selection to choose from — and on the sheet listing the captions, indicate which ones you think are most important to the article.

It is often possible to get free photographs from businesses, organisations or government departments. If you approach anyone for photographs you should always make it quite clear what you will do with them, why you need them and where they are likely to be published. Your first point of contact will usually be the public relations officer, marketing manager or information officer of the organisation concerned.

Do not accept payment from publishers for photographs that you have received free, and always credit them to the originating organisation. It is your responsibility, not the editor's, to make sure any copyright photographs you submit have acknowledgements and/or are paid for in a proper manner.

In cases where you require photographs of objects, art work, etc., in private or public collections, you should approach the owner or curator. Copyright may not exist on the object itself, but it may exist on photographs. In most cases, a request to photograph something will not be turned down (although a small fee may be payable); in some cases, an enquiry to the person concerned may turn up good, usable photographs already in existence.

Digital cameras

Sales of digital cameras now exceed those of their traditional counterparts and are in turn being challenged by the rise in popularity of mobile phones with 1.3 megapixel cameras capable of taking good quality photographs. A good digital camera, together with a quality laser printer and the right photographic paper, can produce photos that are as good as those shot with a film camera. There's no film or processing required, because digital cameras use tiny removable memory cards to store their images, allowing you to view your snaps on your computer before deciding which ones, if any, you wish to print for posterity. Many also offer extra features like burst (fast sequence) modes, 360-degree panorama shooting, time-lapse photography, movie and sound recording, and the ability to store multiple images for slide-show presentations. Perhaps one of the best reasons for switching to a digital camera is that you can take shot after shot without worrying about the cost, allowing you to experiment and be creative without blowing the budget on film and processing costs. And you don't need to worry about whether you've bought the right sort of film or not — the digital camera's clever electronics will automatically balance different colour qualities of light.

Unlike conventional cameras that require film to record pictures, a digital camera's imaging surface is made up of rows of tiny sensors that capture colour and light information which is then converted into digital data, called pixels, that form a photograph. The total sensor array of most digital cameras is called a charge-coupled device (CCD). The more sensors that can be packed onto the CCD's surface, the higher the resolution will be, resulting in a final image with a high pixel count and finer detail. Most digital cameras now offer resolutions in the Megapixel (Mp) range, with 5-plus mega-pixel cameras accounting for the greatest number of sales.

How to choose the right digital camera for your needs

Resolution is obviously an important consideration. To get large images that equal conventional photo-print quality, you must start with enough pixels so your image remains smooth — you don't want to be able to see individual pixels. In film photography, it's the equivalent of blowing an image up to a point where grain becomes noticeable. Digital cameras with less than a million pixels will give you good 10 x 15 cm (4 x 6 inch) snapshots. But for larger prints, you'll need a megapixel camera.

Problems start when you come to print a large image that has been shot with a low-resolution camera. The lower the number of pixels, the bigger each pixel becomes as the print size increases, to the stage where you begin to see each individual pixel and the image starts to disintegrate. If there were more pixels (higher resolution) to begin with, they could spread out to give you a bigger print, yet each one would still be small enough to be invisible to the naked eye.

Another consideration is the light sensitivity setting. Just like conventional films that offer different sensitivities to light, a good-quality digital camera will have multiple light sensitivity settings ranging from ISO 100 to 1000 and the latest models offer a huge range of automatic and overdrive functions. The higher the ISO, the 'grainier' the picture will be. Most digital cameras take perfectly fine pictures under low-light conditions because their lens apertures are reasonably fast (usually around f-2.8). And as a standard feature, most have a built-in flash for really dark conditions and for filling in deep shadows on sunlit, high-contrast subjects. When it comes to freezing action, some even have shutter speeds up to 1/10,000th of a second!

When considering buying a digital camera, the same rules apply as if buying a computer — decide what you want the camera for, how 'high-tech' you want it to be, then talk to a professional supplier and shop around for the best deal.

Drawings, diagrams and other art work

Illustrations other than photographs are almost always commissioned by an editor, except where the writers themselves have particular expertise in that area. If complicated or technical diagrams are required to accompany the body of your text, you should draft a clear black and white pencil sketch indicating what is needed and where it should go, and a caption for any diagrams or drawings should also be composed. Your sketch should include all the elements essential for the final diagram or drawing, and it should be clear enough for a designer or draughtsperson to work from without any confusion.

Unless you have confidence in your own ability as an artist, you should not worry about submitting finished art work with your writing. Many publishers, in the case of children's books for instance, prefer to read the text and visualise for themselves what is required for illustration and what form and style the final illustrations should take. While you may make suggestions about art work, most publishing companies will have a team of experienced designers on hand and it is better to leave the final decisions to them. In the event of serious disagreement about illustration or cover design, most publishers will be happy to negotiate a compromise; it's in their interests to keep all parties happy.

6 Writing for a Market

Analysing the market

Writing for profit can be seen in simple economic terms as a match between supply and demand. The marketplace in which this exchange takes place is very one-sided because there are far more articles written than there are publications in which to print them. You must therefore target the places where your writing is most likely to sell. The directory sections of this book will give you some idea of what is wanted by editors in New Zealand, and where it is wanted — but the in-depth research is up to you.

Getting an idea of whether or not you will be wasting your time writing for a particular outlet is not difficult. A simple process of deduction will give you some basic information. Firstly, is the magazine or newspaper in the market for freelance contributions? You can decide this by a process of elimination. Check the regular features and note their subjects. The editor will not want someone duplicating work that is presumably already being done competently. Next, look through two or three recent copies of your target publication. How many of the articles have been written by staff writers? (Check the contributors' list, and compare names over all your issues.) How many stories are left? These could well have been written by freelance writers. Note their content, style and length, and ask yourself if you could tailor your own submissions to this general format.

Work out who reads the magazine or newspaper. The editor must know what his or her readers want in a publication, and so must you if you want to supply something that meets that demand. Are the advertisements expensive-looking? (That often means better payments are available to freelance contributors.) Are they aimed at a particular type of person? A particular age group? Advertisers, too, must know exactly who they are reaching with their promotional dollars. Once you have a clear picture of the readership of a publication, you will know if your writing will appeal to them, or whether you can alter your writing style to create a niche for yourself in that market.

Look through the publication, and find out if it actively encourages freelance contributors, or offers payments for submissions. Is it a new publication? If so, payment may not be high, but you could establish yourself as a regular contributor. Think like an editor, and search for ways in which the magazine could be better, i.e., ways in which your articles could enhance the publication.

If you are marketing a book manuscript, check out the directory section in this book first, and then go to your local bookshop or library. Look through the New Zealand section, and see which publishers handle books similar in nature to yours. Search through magazines that regularly feature book reviews to see if you can detect which publishers might be in the market for a new idea. Browse through the bibliographies of books similar to yours, and note who publishes in your area of interest. Make a list of possible publishers, and order them according to who might be the best bet. Approach the first publisher on your list, and if he or she is not interested, keep working through the names until you find one who is — or until you get a clear signal that you are wasting your time. Always be ready to accept that a project may not work, and know when to start something new instead.

What does an editor look for?

Newspapers and magazines

Your manuscript has reached the top of the editor's in-tray. It is well presented and has a clean, professional look to it; now the merits of your writing must appeal to the person who will accept or reject your submission.

An editor's first question will be 'Why should I publish this?' He or she will be persuaded to do so only by work that shows quality in three main areas: content, readability and impact. If you have written your article, and appraised it with the same mental checklist as your potential editor, your chances of success will be greatly enhanced.

Content

A good article is based around solid content. It contains factual information; it has an interpretation of that information; there is a balanced viewpoint; and the article either raises new ideas or treats old ones in a fresh, original way. Try to keep the following questions in your mind as you write:

- are the facts correct?
- have you used authoritative sources?
- are the facts organised in a way that draws the reader on?
- are the facts analysed and interpreted in a clear, commonsense way?
- are the facts and the interpretation brought together in a coherent fashion?
- are opinions and facts clearly distinguished?
- are conflicting opinions presented?
- does the article treat the subject in a new or different way?
- does the article present you as someone who knows the topic?

Readability

Any article must make its readers want to go on, by challenging them, by making them ask questions and by capturing and sustaining their attention and interest. It must not be a chore to read, nor should it use language in a gimmicky or clichéd fashion, and it should be written in a tone which is appropriate to both the subject and the audience. Your readability checklist should run something like this:

- will the article appeal to readers of the target publication?
- will it invite readers to identify with the article?
- is it free of jargon?
- does it get to the point?
- does your own voice come through as intelligent and authoritative?
- is the article written using active, rather than passive, construction?
- will readers find the language appropriate?
- does the article use a friendly, conversational tone where this is needed?
- is the writing free of any gimmick or device which may disrupt the flow of information to its readers?
- does the article flow well when read aloud?

Impact

An article must have more effect than the mere imparting of information or opinion. It must also leave readers thinking, offer them new understandings, and foster, extend or challenge their interest. Ask yourself the following questions:

- does the article offer readers something they hadn't thought about before?
- will the article leave readers feeling they have gained something from reading it?
- is the article written in a strong enough way to leave some impression?
- is the article written in a contemporary style?
- is the article relevant to readers' current interests?

Magazine and newspaper editors will be asking these questions as they themselves become the first readers of your manuscript. They know the tastes and preferences of their own readers, and have an obligation to make sure each article they publish has 'yes' answers to all the above. If you run through them all yourself, before submitting an article, you may well pick up areas that could be improved — before it's too late.

Books

A book editor's first thought, while reading through a manuscript, is usually 'will it sell?'. In your proposal, query letter or covering letter, you must therefore try to set out the reasons why you think it will. Before you begin, put yourself in the place of a book editor, and check through the following points:

Subject
Is the topic or scope of your book in line with the publisher's present list, i.e., do they publish books of this sort? Is it a subject that will appeal to a wide New Zealand audience, or is it a minority interest? Has the publisher had successes with other books of a similar nature?

Need
Is your book needed? Will your book be bought for interest or because it's essential for people to own a copy? Does your book say anything new? Have similar books had success overseas?

Competition
Are there any other books on this subject? Are they written in a New Zealand context? Are they widely used, or out of date? Is the book going to need a lot of money spent on its promotion in a competitive market, e.g., cookbooks or gardening books?

Audience
Who is your book aimed at? How many people are likely to buy it? Is your manuscript written in a style appropriate to this audience? Will the final cover price be perceived as reasonable?

Distribution
Will the major bookselling chains take your book? Will it require a high promotional budget? Where will it be reviewed, and in what light?

Author
Are you qualified to write this book? Have you got a track record, either in book writing, or in the subject itself, which will inspire confidence in the reader (and editor)?

Cost
How many pages is your book going to be? Will it need illustrations, or colour photographs or expensive design and production? Is it fiction or non-fiction? (Fiction is usually cheaper to typeset.) Will it need a full-colour jacket? What sort of paper will the book need? Can it be printed in New Zealand, or will it have to be sent to China or elsewhere offshore?

Revenue
Is the book likely to make a profit in New Zealand? Does it have potential for sales overseas? How long is it likely to keep selling for?

If the answers to all these questions look satisfactory (and your manuscript was an enjoyable or interesting read), the editor will start doing some sums. A simple example of the basic process is outlined opposite:

Based on prior experience, and taking into account the cost of production, the editor will decide on a probable print run of, say, 3000 copies (an average run for a New Zealand book). With a balance of optimism and pessimism, the editor expects eighty per cent of the print run to sell — 2400 copies. Other books of a similar style sell for about $29.95; on each of these copies, the author will typically receive a ten per cent royalty, and booksellers will typically expect a discount of at least forty per cent. The editor estimates the book will cost about $3,000 for typesetting, design and cover artwork; the cost of the paper, printing and binding for a print run of 3000 works out at, say, $4 per copy.

With these figures, the editor works out the net sales income:

Price received	=	cover price ($29.95)	–	retail discount (40%)	= $17.97
Net sales income	=	net per copy ($17.97)	x	copies sold (2,400)	= $43,128

Next, the editor works on the other side of the sum: direct costs.

Typesetting and design costs ($3,000) + unit costs (3000 copies @ $4 each; $12,000) + royalty (10% of 2400 copies sold at $29.95; $7,188) = $22,188.

The gross profit the publishing company can expect is the difference: $20,940. If the work is not going to be edited in-house, this cost will also need to be allowed for and out of this the editor must also take overheads, such as salaries, distribution costs, sales commission, advertising costs and administration costs, usually figured at about thirty per cent of net sales income. As this comes to $12,938.40, the net profit is $8,001.60.

The final question is 'Is it worthwhile doing?' To work out the return on its investment, the publishing house divides the net profit by the total costs. Thus:

8002 : (22,188 + 12,938) = 0.23

This figure of 0.23 represents twenty-three per cent, and is the publisher's return on investment. If your book can be expected to provide that sort of a return or better to a publishing company, they'll be pleased to receive your manuscript for assessment. Anything less than fifteen per cent, and they are better off keeping their overdraft under tighter control, until someone with a better proposition comes along . . .

Why does an editor use a freelance writer?

The advantage of using freelance writers in preference to permanent staff usually comes down to one thing — economy. The cost of buying a one-off article is much less than employing someone on a full-time basis, and using freelancers also allows an editor to choose from a wide range of people and writing styles. A flat rate or agreed sum can be budgeted by an editor, and there are no further hassles for either party.

Editors may choose to use a freelance writer on jobs that come up infrequently, such as quarterly publications, where employing others on a full-time basis or diverting other in-house staff would be uneconomic. They may, on occasion, require specialist knowledge for a feature or in-depth article; and an editor may also like to try something new in his or her publication, without taking the risk of actually employing someone.

Freelance writers will find that their work generally falls into two categories: that which is prepared and sent to an editor on speculation, taking a chance it will be rejected; and work which has been commissioned by an editor before writing begins. The latter requires careful preparation before any writing proceeds.

Freelance writers commissioned by an editor should always ensure that they know:

- the amount they will be paid
- the deadlines they need to meet
- a contact person within the magazine or newspaper whom they can approach for help or information
- how often the editor wishes to be updated on the progress of the work
- exactly what is required in the article, in terms of length, magazine style, etc.
- any background information or contacts the editor may have for the topic.

Remember that being commissioned to write is no guarantee that your work will be published. Obviously, an editor will have some confidence in your work before he or she approaches you, but sometimes, for any number of reasons, a story will simply have to be dropped. Be sure that both you and the editor are agreed on a 'kill' fee, or payment for the work you have put in, regardless of whether the writing is used or not. You and your editor want the same thing — a successful story — so don't leave anything in doubt.

7 Writing for Children

New Zealanders' love of reading starts when they are very small. Indeed, despite the statistics we sometimes hear, our literacy rates in the early years of school are amongst the highest in the world. This is in no small way due to an emphasis on teaching children to read through a maximum exposure to print at a very early age. Children are fortunate in New Zealand in that they are encouraged to enjoy as wide a range of styles and genres and categories of writing as possible right from the start.

In the classroom and out of the classroom, New Zealand children are also fortunate in the wide range of extremely high quality local books they have access to. New Zealand's children's book publishers are on a par with the best anywhere, and this is reflected in the huge export business that has grown around children's publishing. Led by small independent publishing houses, the children's book segment of the publishing industry is now a multimillion-dollar industry in its own right, and the returns for authors who can capture young imaginations with a few well-chosen words can be very good indeed.

As always, there's a catch. If there wasn't, everybody would be a children's author. The catch is that almost everyone who attempts a children's story gets it wrong. They get it wrong because they look at children's books, some with only thirty or forty words over eight pages, and think how easy it must be. What they don't see is that in an adult novel, the author has some two to three hundred pages to create a mood, introduce characters and tell a story with a start, middle and end. In children's books, you have none of the leeway that a writer for adults has. You are also dealing with an audience that has a limited capability for processing both words and concepts. Children's writing is, in fact, one of the most difficult styles to get right. It's a little like coming up with the prize-winning entry in a promotional competition — in less than forty words, tell us what happened, why, where, how and who to. Oh, and don't forget to make it emotive, imaginative and interesting enough for a child to want to do the hard work of reading through it.

The following notes will give you an understanding of the essential elements of writing successfully for children — and also list a few dos and don'ts.

The story

Many of us forget what hard work it was to actually read through a whole book when we were young children. Some of us probably still find it hard work to read through a whole book, for more or less the same reasons. The story is dull or slow-moving; there are too many words and not enough action; sometimes, we may not even understand the words or the context that they are used in; perhaps the characters don't inspire any reaction from the reader; or maybe it's simply not about what we're interested in.

If you are going to write for children, you have a very critical audience to cope with. The books they want to read must have a quality text, worthy of the effort. The subject matter, or the theme, must be about something that interests children, something that they can relate to easily. It is often important, although not essential, for some of the characters in the story to be in some way like the children, so they can establish an empathy with what is happening to the characters. Most importantly, there must be a point to reading the story: like any adult, the child expects a beginning (where things are introduced), a middle (where things happen) and an end (where the conflict or events or interactions come to a conclusion, or a twist in the tale is experienced).

Know your audience

Authors should make every effort to try to find out what actually interests children in the age group they are aiming for. It is almost certainly different from what the authors were interested in when they were children, and this is a common failing for aspiring children's writers: they write about what they think children want to read about. Children today grow up and live in a very different world from the one that existed ten, twenty or thirty years ago. What may appear to be new technology for adults, such as CDs, the Internet, and interactive computer games, are things that have been around for the entire lifetime of a child. Respect the knowledge and capabilities of your audience at all times, and never write down to children.

Be aware, too, that in New Zealand we have an extremely diverse population of children who want good books to read. Certainly, there are a good number of white, middle-class families out there — but there are also Maori children, Pacific Island children, Vietnamese children, Indian children and Muslim children. There are children who have various degrees of physical ability or disability, depending on the words you prefer to use; there are children who find it hard to read because of various family or social pressures. All these children need characters and stories that they can relate to.

Lastly, always remember that the most successful children's books often work on more than one level, appealing to the child in every adult as well as the children themselves. After all, it is usually the parents or teachers who have to dig into their pockets to satisfy the demand for good children's material. They have to like the story.

Text structure

In children's publishing, there are three generally accepted levels of difficulty, which children tend to move through as they gain competency in the reading process. These levels are emergent, early, and fluency.

If you are writing for very young readers, you need to be aware of the kinds of text structures that they are able to handle. These include:

- structurally repetitive one-line captions at the very early level, moving on to two- or three-line sentences as competency grows
- high frequency vocabulary, dealing with familiar objects and events
- predictable language, sometimes with direct speech
- occasional changes in word order at higher levels
- oral language structures predominate.

Early readers who have had some exposure to print, and who have successfully mastered the above, move on to:

- four-line sentences
- a reasonable number of new words per page may be introduced
- examination of familiar objects and actions
- introduction of pure non-fiction forms
- varied sentence patterns, including repeated phrases or refrains
- imaginative, abstract or unfamiliar concepts
- rhyme and cumulative storylines.

Fluent readers need books of varied content and style. Books may introduce challenging vocabulary, and may include advanced text structures and common book concepts, such as diagrams, maps, flow charts, etc. Extended descriptions and elaborated episodes can be introduced.

Don't be bound by the above notes, however. Do your market research as fully as you can. You'll find that children don't mention any of the points we've listed here. The essential elements of creativity, imagination and the sheer enjoyment of a good story are the really important ones for that most discerning of audiences.

Formats

Picture book formats usually start out at eight pages. They then rise to 12 pages, 16 pages, 24 pages, and upwards in regular steps. Authors writing for a limited number of pages (say 8–16) should present their text paginated so the publisher can immediately see how the story develops from page to page. One of the most common mistakes budding children's writers make is to assume that an eight-page book means eight pages of text. Good children's books, like good adult books, always have a title page! With such limited space, if an editor has to discard a line to make the manuscript fit a format, it can destroy the feel or rhythm of the entire story.

Illustrations

Most publishers of children's stories prefer to use professional illustrators to work on new titles, because if you think getting the words right is difficult, then children's book illustration has twice as many potential pitfalls. You may, of course, need to submit descriptions of action, or simple line drawings to explain particular passages of text, and this is quite acceptable. Unless you are very confident that your artistic ability is of a very high standard, don't spend a lot of time and effort working on illustrations for your work.

Royalties

Because illustrating children's books is very precise, always demanding and certainly time-consuming, it can also be very expensive. Generally, it is accepted that the publisher should commission and pay for the art work that they use in a children's title. Because of this expense (as opposed to adult publishing, where the author is usually expected to provide photographs or illustrations), children's publishers typically offer a lower royalty to authors. A fair royalty for a children's picture book would be in the range of five to six per cent of price received, sometimes higher for established writers. Be wary of publishers who only offer a flat fee for using your work. While the sum may be attractive to start with, the publisher will be reaping the benefit of sales long after your rights cheque has gone. Remember that many children's books are exported in large numbers; and also that a successful children's book can have growing sales for many years. Be careful, too, of publishers who offer a fee for one-time use in periodicals or books, but who are reluctant to then release the rights to use your material in other places. You could be losing future potential income if you don't check your contracts carefully. A useful guide is *Writing and Illustrating for Children*, published annually by Christchurch City Libraries and available for $5.00 plus $1.00 post and packing (P.O. Box 1466, Christchurch Mail Centre, Christchurch 8140; email library@ccc.govt.nz). Copies are available in the reference section of all city libraries. It outlines major publishing outlets for children's writing and specific publishers' guidelines to authors. Many good children's publishers will provide their own guidelines for authors at no cost to prospective writers.

8 Writing for Overseas Markets

Overseas opportunities

If you can sell material to publishers in New Zealand, there is no reason to ignore the opportunities that exist in overseas markets. New Zealand newspapers, magazines and books are of a high quality compared to those that flourish beyond our shores so, if your writing is good enough for them, it should be equally attractive to buyers in other countries. The small market in New Zealand means that, to succeed in competition with imported titles, New Zealand publishers can afford to take only the very best. New Zealand writers, too, are fortunate in sharing the same language as the three biggest overseas markets — Australia, United Kingdom and North America.

As with domestic writing, the key to getting your work in print is knowing the market. Writing tailored to a specific publisher will sell, but merely attempting to sell your rejected New Zealand manuscripts overseas will end up costing you a lot of postage and time for little return. Writing for overseas publication means working with subjects that can fall into three categories: those with universal appeal; those with a specialist or technical aspect that will appeal to readers regardless of nationality; and those stories with a regional or national character.

Writing about New Zealand, if it is directed specifically to a foreign audience, can be very successful when it is written for the 'universal appeal' bracket. Often, overseas magazines and newspapers are good buyers of what is to them interesting or unusual overseas feature material, in which New Zealand is portrayed as a distant and exotic place. There is a great deal of interest in this country. The good writer can tap into this and find a niche which will often prove to be profitable and satisfying.

Finding a market

Never has it been so easy to research overseas markets. With the advent of the Internet, a comprehensive listing of major publishing houses anywhere in the world is a mouse-click away. Major media and publishing directories are available in the reference sections of most big libraries; other smaller libraries may be able to interloan material for you. Because there are obvious difficulties in getting hold of copies of many overseas publications (and in the case of foreign language editions, reading them), these international directories can be invaluable for targeting your market. Ask your librarian to advise you on the best way to consult any of the directories listed below.

The Writer's Handbook, published annually by Macmillan/PEN, London.
This publication, easily spotted with its bright yellow cover, provides a full guide to all United Kingdom publishers, along with a brief outline of the bigger European publishing houses. It also provides good coverage of other outlets for writing in the United Kingdom and Europe, including radio, television, stage and film.

Writers' and Artists' Yearbook, published annually by A & C Black, London.
This publication details British markets and also offers a basic coverage of other Commonwealth markets for writing, artwork and photography. While your first sale to an overseas publisher will cover the cost of buying a copy, these guides can be consulted in most public libraries if you do not wish to purchase your own. Be sure, however, that you are consulting an up-to-date copy.

Literary Market Place, published annually by Bowker, New York.
A comprehensive directory of American book publishing, available in the reference section of main city libraries.

Magazine Industry Market Place, published annually by Bowker, New York.
A complete list of every periodical in America, along with brief details of their editorial requirements.

Willings Press Guide, published annually by British Media Publications, East Grinstead.
A complete directory of the British press and the principal publications of Europe, the United States, Australasia, the Far East, Africa and the Middle East. You can also subscribe online at www.willingspress.com

Benn's Media Directory, published annually by Benn, Tonbridge.
One of the oldest directories, this publication comes in three editions, one covering the UK, one covering Europe, and the third covering the rest of the world. A very comprehensive directory.

Writers' and Photographers' Marketing Guide, published every two years by the Australian Writers' Professional Service.
A particularly good directory for Australian and New Zealand writers and photographers.

While you are in your library browsing through these directories, take some time to check through the periodicals section. Some libraries subscribe to a number of overseas magazines and journals, and checking these can be an easy and cheap way of familiarising yourself with the needs and tastes of overseas editors. Many of the larger booksellers and newsagents also stock foreign newspapers and magazines and, although these may be expensive to buy, you can be sure you will be facing a lot of domestic competition in trying to sell articles to them. Therefore money spent on research should be regarded as an investment.

Overseas markets offer good opportunities for multiple sales in different countries; a good story that sells in the United States may also be saleable in Great Britain after some small adjustments in style have been made. When submitting manuscripts, make it clear that you are offering first serial rights for that country only; and be reasonable about to whom, or how many publishers, you submit. There is little to be gained from annoying editors who run your story only to find it appearing in a widely-read imported magazine of the same nature.

New Zealand writers should bear in mind that an often ignored market of huge proportions exists in their region — Southeast Asia. Large-circulation English language publications exist throughout that area, particularly in Hong Kong, Singapore, and Taiwan. Often newspapers and magazines from these countries will accept articles about New Zealand or the South Pacific, especially if they can be tied in with items of local interest, such as immigration or business opportunities. India and Africa, too, support a large number of English language publications, but submitting to editors in these regions can be fraught with difficulty — use them only as a last-ditch option, and don't hold your breath waiting for a response.

Overseas agents

Instead of trying to analyse large numbers of expensive foreign publications and then carefully targeting prospective markets, you may wish to consider approaching a foreign press agent willing to do this for you. Foreign agents have the advantage of knowing their own countries and markets intimately, and because they depend on selling your material for their own income, you can be assured that if they accept your writing they will be trying hard to sell it. Updated lists of foreign agents in various countries can be found in the *Writers' and Artists' Yearbook* and also in Macmillan's *Writer's Handbook*.

Usually, a writer will write to an agent, saying he or she is interested in selling work to a particular territory, outlining his or her writing experience (and successes) domestically, stating a specific area of expertise or interest and offering to send a selection of sample pieces for the agent to consider. If an agent is interested in working with you, he or she will detail commission rates, payment details and other requirements. Usually, payment is by means of a monthly or bi-monthly account, itemising materials received and sold or rejected.

There are, of course, a number of New Zealand publishers who market their books overseas as well, so if you have an idea for an international book you need not necessarily go offshore to do your business. The publishers of this book, David Bateman Ltd, for example, have a sizeable programme of international books marketed throughout the world, and many New Zealand publishers are subsidiaries of overseas firms or have other close links with foreign publishers and distributors. Children's books are another area where international possibilities always exist. Print runs of 20,000 are not uncommon for a good New Zealand children's book, most of which are exported to markets in North America and the United Kingdom.

Presentation

If you prefer to handle your own marketing, be prepared for sometimes lengthy delays while editors consider and reply to your manuscripts or query letters. It can be frustrating wondering just what happened to that submission you sent off months ago, so do your utmost to speed the process. Always enclose enough International Reply Coupons to ensure an airmail reply, and staple these to your SAE (they will be processed as international stamps). Always enclose an airmail envelope, just to make sure foreign post offices process your mail as airmail. If you find yourself submitting material to one or more countries on a regular basis, you may find it economical to write to the philatelic bureau in that country requesting details about purchasing stamps of an appropriate value.

If it is not important that your actual manuscript be returned to you (it can be expensive paying full postage both ways), make sure you state that fact clearly in your covering letter — but also make it clear that you wish to receive notification if it is rejected. Another way of reducing postage costs is to include a small 'this manuscript was rejected' card, addressed to yourself and filled in with the title of your work. The editor can simply drop it into the post and, again, you will not be left wondering if anyone has actually received your submission on the other side of the world. If you have an email address, include this with other contact details so that publishers can easily acknowledge receipt of your work, or contact you regarding any queries.

Always make sure that you include 'New Zealand' on any addresses you give your prospective editor (on title pages especially), and, if you normally include a contact telephone number on your submissions, add the full STD code as well. It is unlikely you will get a call at three o'clock in the morning (afternoon tea time there . . .) but it does no harm to appear eager and available for contact. If overseas publishers do get in contact with you, always reply straight away. You are battling against the perception of distance when you try to sell material overseas, so proving that you are easily accessible makes a lot of difference.

Extra effort should always be given to presentation. You're working in competition with local writers in their own territories, and this immediately gives them an edge. Use good, sturdy A4 envelopes. They will cost more to post, but your manuscript will look that little bit better when it arrives on the editor's desk. Don't be tempted to use bank or airmail paper either — stay with the paper weights you would normally use when submitting in New Zealand. Work into your covering letter an offer to do other work of any kind that the editor may consider putting your way. He or she may not be able to use your article, but may just be searching for a regular correspondent from this part of the world. There is no harm in trying.

Try to avoid sending photographs or illustrations until you have a firm offer from overseas publishers (unless they are essential to the article). Always offer to supply illustrations if you can, however, especially if you are writing on a New Zealand or South Pacific topic that the editor may have difficulty illustrating from his or her own resources. You should make every effort to help, otherwise your idea might end up in the 'interesting, but too hard' basket. If you feel photographs and illustrations would enhance your chances on the first approach, consider sending good photocopies instead of originals.

If you are sending original or rare photographs or transparencies, consider using a courier. It's often easier trying to trace missing packages through them than the overseas postal services. Also, you should think about using couriers when submitting time-sensitive material to publishers outside Europe, the United Kingdom and Australia. The postal services in the United States and in Canada can be very slow, sometimes up to four or five weeks for airmail delivery; those in less-developed countries can be even worse.

Comb your writing for colloquialisms and New Zealand words and brand names. What may seem perfectly sensible to you may be unintelligible to others overseas, especially if you are submitting in English to foreign language publications. If you are in any doubt, substitute another word. Check spelling variations as well. In Australia and Great Britain you will generally find similar styles, but the United States can be tricky. Reading your target publication will, of course, alert you to some specific house rules. The *Chicago Manual of Style*, available in larger libraries, is generally accepted as a good base for US style.

Most publishers in Europe will accept manuscripts if they are written in English, and will have staff available to translate them into their domestic languages. An agent will sometimes offer this service to increase his or her own revenue. A small percentage of your fee will be deducted for translation in these cases. Never attempt a translation yourself, unless you are certain of your own fluency.

Payment

You probably won't make a lot of money writing for the overseas market, but you should at least aim to cover the cost of all the articles you have had rejected overseas. Unless you wish to make a concerted effort, overseas sales should be seen as something extra to try once in a while. The sales are good, and having foreign credits in your clippings file can be advantageous.

Foreign magazines will always pay at their normal domestic rates for submissions from New Zealand, usually in their own currency. Some magazines will make the effort to pay in New Zealand dollars, but don't worry if you get foreign currency cheques. Cheques in most major currencies can be deposited directly into New Zealand accounts, after conversion by the foreign teller at your usual trading bank. It is wise to keep a note of the cheque number, issuing bank, account number and sum; the simplest way is to photocopy each payment as you receive it. It may also be a good idea (depending on how much you earn from overseas sales) to keep a separate file of all overseas payments received for tax purposes. Although they do not always make it clear, some overseas publishers deduct a sum equal to their own domestic tax rate from payments to writers. If this has already been done, you need pay no further tax on it in New Zealand.

If in doubt, ask your publisher — he or she will be happy to answer your query.

9 Contracts

You may write primarily for the love of writing, but you might as well be in it for what money there is. As outlined in the Introduction, publishing is a business, and that wonderful document every aspiring writer dreams of, a publishing contract, is a business agreement. It is a legal document that sets down obligations that both you and the publisher must fulfil, so it is therefore important to read and understand what is often a lengthy and complicated piece of writing. Don't be put off by the jargon in it, and don't be afraid to ask your publisher (or an independent person) about any parts of it that you do not understand. Before you sign, remember that all contracts are negotiable. Nothing is set until your signature appears on the bottom line.

Rights

The book you have written is yours, and yours alone. It belongs to no one else. A publisher may say 'yes' to the idea of publishing it but, by virtue of copyright law, the actual material belongs to you. You therefore have the right to decide how that material may be used — and the first part of a contract that you should examine is the part that details what you are giving the publisher permission to do.

Initially, look at whether or not the contract allows you to retain these important rights. There are few cases where it is to the author's advantage to assign copyright to anyone else. Generally, a contract should be a licence to publish, not a licence to transfer ownership of the material. Where this occurs, you are transferring the right to earn anything more from your work. This may not be a very sensible idea, although it may be worth your while if you have been commissioned to write something and are being paid in full on delivery.

The length of time for which you are granting a licence to publish is also negotiable in most cases. Where the licence is granted for 'the full term of copyright', that in effect means your lifetime. If you are happy with that, by all means agree to it. If not, talk with your publisher. In many instances, the publisher retains the licence to publish while a work is in print and if, for whatever reason, a decision is made not to reprint a work, relevant clauses in the contract deal with the process of publishing rights reverting to an author.

Contracts will also specify a 'territory' for which the licence to publish is given. This may be world-wide, or it may be for New Zealand. Think about your book before granting world-wide rights. If it is of universal appeal, does your publisher have the facilities to sell it overseas? Or would you be better off granting them New Zealand rights only, and perhaps approaching a publisher in Australia, the United States or Great Britain for overseas rights? Don't sign away your rights before finding out what your publisher intends doing with respect to the book's potential overseas. If you think your work has potential overseas, ask your publisher what arrangements he or she may have with overseas publishing companies. Often even small New Zealand companies will have long-standing arrangements with overseas publishers, and may well be able to make bulk sales of your work to them.

A clause on rights may also cover the following situations: serial rights; translation rights; film rights; dramatic, stage and television rights; mechanical copying rights; various digital or electronic rights including CD-ROM and on-line rights; merchandising rights; book club rights; cartoon rights; and reprint rights for different publishers. You are under no obligation to give these rights to your publisher, but if you do (in many cases, they can negotiate better payments for you than you can on your own) be sure you receive a fair percentage of the sale of each of these rights. Percentages vary, but are usually from fifty to ninety per cent, depending on the type and potential.

Delivery of the manuscript

A contract will usually specify a date by which you must hand over the manuscript — unless you have already done so. Think about whether or not you can do the work required in the time available. If not, most publishers will be happy to amend the date for delivery of the manuscript.

Other matters

Indexes, illustrations, photographs, maps, etc., which are needed for the book, may be the responsibility of the author. Check that the amount and scope of any other matter you are required to supply is reasonable. Usually it will be your responsibility to clear copyright on any material you may wish to use. Contracts usually specify the format the work will be published in – size, binding, paper quality, extent. It is particularly important to check these details and make sure you are happy with the publisher's proposed format for books which have a lot of illustrations or photographs as such details will affect the quality of the published work.

Corrections

It is expensive to change large passages of text of a book after it has been typeset, so most publishers protect themselves by inserting a clause outlining just how many changes can be made to a draft after it has been set. The manuscript you submit should be in as close a form to the final as you can make it. But if you are prone to making large numbers of alterations at a late stage, check your responsibilities under the contract; you will generally be liable for the cost of excessive changes.

Legal matters

Every contract will have a clause in which you promise not to defame anyone or breach copyright. The clause may also specify what will happen if the publisher's legal advisors consider that your book does contain matter of dubious legal standing; it may also specify who should do what in the event of things coming to court. Read carefully, and don't take responsibility for anything you don't understand.

Revision

Your book may be a great success and sell out within weeks — and the publisher may decide to print another edition, with a few small changes. A revision clause sets out the way in which further work, such as updating the text, is to be done, and specifies who is to do it. In most cases, you will want to do it yourself. If you do, make sure that is spelt out.

Publication

The publisher may have said yes, but a guarantee to actually publish your book should be included in the contract. This clause should say when the publisher will publish your book (you don't want them sitting on your manuscript for more than twelve months); it should say how widely they will distribute the book; and it should give other details, e.g., how much they will expect to sell it for and how large a first print run they will be making. These things have obvious consequences for your royalty cheques.

It is also useful to have a clause protecting your rights and payments in the case of your publisher ceasing business. Does the contract set out what will happen to your book if someone else buys the publishing company or if it goes broke? In the latter case, the safest option is for all rights, licences, etc., to be returned to you.

Presentation copies

You should reasonably expect to get some copies (usually between six and ten) of your own book for free. Many contracts make provision for further copies to be purchased at a special author's rate.

Advances

If you need some money to complete your book, or for any other reason, you can try to negotiate an advance on your royalties with the publisher. This is usually a set sum, which will be deducted from your royalty earnings once the book is selling. Don't be greedy — if your advance exceeds royalties, you may be asked to pay the balance back, although this is a rare occurrence. You are generally expected to use your advance to help out with manuscript development costs, such as the cost of getting illustrations or collating information. It is not the done thing to spend your entire advance and then go back to the publisher and ask for more — so prepare a fairly detailed budget for yourself before broaching the subject. Likewise, if there is to be little or no expenditure on your part before you can deliver the manuscript, be sensible in any demands you make for advances. It can be a long time after contracting before the publisher sees any return on his or her investment.

Royalties

This clause sets out how much you will be paid for your book. Royalties can be based on the recommended retail price, most often 10 per cent of this amount, or increasingly on the price the publisher receives (the net price). The percentage on the latter varies. Even if the royalty is based on what the book is likely to be sold to the public for, exclusive of GST, when volume sales (typically 500–1000 or more copies) are made, e.g., to bookseller chains, book clubs, or to overseas publishers for distribution in other countries, the royalty percentage reverts to being on the price the publisher receives.

Make sure you are clear about the royalty and how it is calculated. Net price can be calculated after the publisher's distribution and sales costs have been deducted, thereby significantly reducing royalty returns. Ask for a definition of the net price and an approximation of what this might be for your book.

Most contracts will also list various other possibilities for publication, such as in anthologies, or paperback, or in cheap editions. Make sure you are happy with the figure the publisher proposes to pay you in each case, and remember that it is only a proposition until you sign the contract. Ask for more if you think your royalty rate is too low.

Many contracts also include separate royalty rates for overseas sales, which are often at a much lower percentage than domestic sales. If you think your work has a good chance of achieving overseas sales, it may be worthwhile adding a clause leaving this part of the contract open for negotiation if and when an overseas sale is achieved so that the royalty rate reflects the size of the print run and other variables.

Children's books tend to be an exception to the rule. This is because the publisher generally finds or commissions illustrations, and pays for these separately. For this reason, royalty rates are generally expected to be lower than for general trade books.

Although most publishers will initially offer only a flat royalty rate, it may be wise to ask for a rising rate if the book sells well. For instance, you could ask that for the first 3000 copies, you be paid 10 per cent; if sales exceed that figure, you get 12 per cent; and if the book proves to be a runaway success, you get even more. Rising rates will not necessarily eat into the publisher's profits, because the unit cost of each book often decreases with an increased print run, especially if the book reprints very soon after first publication. Negotiate.

Remainders

Your contract should make clear what is to happen with any leftover books that do not sell. If they are to be sold at a reduced price, make sure you receive an adequate royalty on these. If they are remaindered at below cost, you should not expect to receive a royalty. You may wish to have first option to purchase your books at the remainder price. This is often included in remainder clauses. Also check that there is a fair period of time specified before a publisher decides to remainder your work. As mentioned in the Rights section above, insist also on a clause specifying how long a book may stay out of print before an author is entitled to approach another publisher with the rights to publish.

Copyright

The publisher should undertake to insert a notice of copyright into your book, making it clear who owns the copyright. In return, you state that the material you are giving the publisher is, in fact, original and your own work. A contract should also detail what is to happen if your own copyright is breached, i.e., who will take legal action? Who will pay for this action? What will happen to the money received from any court proceedings? Where copyright is breached, it is usual for a publisher and author to seek redress jointly. It is usual for the author to obtain, and pay for, any permissions for the use of copyright material in his or her book.

Accounts

The contract should cover accounting matters, such as when your royalties will be paid, where they will be paid and how they will be paid. It is usual for accounts to be made up every six months, and for payment to be made on those six-monthly reconciliations after a further waiting period of between one to three months. There can also be a provision to hold back royalties where sales are on a sale or return basis.

Options

There may be a clause giving your publisher first option on any future work of a similar type that you may produce. You must decide if you wish to grant them the right of first refusal on anything you propose to do in future; or whether you would rather 'shop around'.

Signing

A contract should clearly state what it is for, i.e., the name of the book or publication it deals with. It should also state in unambiguous terms who it is between. Once you are satisfied with all the terms and conditions of a contract, you can sign it wherever the publisher indicates (usually on the last page) — and you should also initial each page. You will have to sign two copies — one is for you to keep and the other is for the publisher. File your copy away in a safe place — it is an important document.

Minimum terms

The New Zealand Society of Authors (formerly PEN, NZ Inc.) produces a model standard contract, entitled *The Business Of Writing*. The full document is available from the NZSA for $10 (members) and $35 (non-members), include $2 for p&p. Send a cheque and self-addressed label to NZSA, PO Box 67013, Mt Eden, Auckland 1349. To join the NZSA, visit their website at www.authors.org.nz and go to 'How to join NZSA' to submit an application. *The Business of Writing* also covers copyright, advances, subsidiary rights, GST status, how to negotiate effectively, and more.

10 New Zealand Copyright

There can be few areas in which the letter of the law is as open to interpretation as it is with regard to writing and publishing. Every situation is different, and for every case where a clear decision appears to have been made, there seems to be another opening up several more questions. You should, however, be aware of the basic rules governing two aspects of your trade — copyright and defamation. In these cases, a little knowledge and common sense will ensure that few problems are encountered.

Copyright

What is copyright?

Once you have written something, even a hand-written page of manuscript, it is regarded as your personal property and may not be copied by anyone else without permission. This right is known as copyright. Copyright covers such things as literature, drama, photography, art, music, recordings, films and broadcasts. What it does not cover are ideas, plots and themes; copyright can exist only on tangible material. It also assumes some degree of creativity or thought, but exactly where the line is drawn can be unclear. Lists of rugby results and team draws are not copyright, but lists of television programmes may be. The title of a book cannot be protected under copyright either.

Where a writer is commissioned to do some work for a newspaper or magazine, a publisher becomes the owner of the right to publish the work (first New Zealand serial rights), but the writer generally retains all other rights, e.g., to publish his or her work later in book form, online, on-sell to another publication (second New Zealand rights) or overseas. Usually all rights to a work are owned by the publishers when someone in their employment writes material for them. In both these cases, the allocation of rights may be altered by a contract of employment or an agreement over conditions of service.

Large magazine publishing houses may request a freelance writer assigns copyright to them, but there is no obligation to do so and writers should seriously consider the implications before agreeing to such requests.

The writer is not required to do anything (apart from write) to be protected by copyright — there are no forms to fill in or people to be notified. (There are, however, certain advantages to be gained by registering a copyright in the United States. If you expect a large market for your work there, write to the Registrar of Copyrights, Library of Congress, Washington, D.C., for forms or further information. Usually your publisher, or the company they market to in the United States, will do all this for you.)

Copyright and its associated legal framework are covered by the Copyright Act 1994 and subsequent Amendments. This Act sets out what copyright means and how it is protected in New Zealand. The following sets out the major points covered by the Act that are specifically relevant to writers. If you want to read the Act yourself, it is available for purchase through some bookshops or a copy will be held in most major libraries.

Protection

In the majority of cases, the copyright to a work belongs to the author for a set number of years, unless that person assigns it to someone else. In New Zealand, if publication occurs during the lifetime of an author, it is protected for fifty years from the end of the year in which he or she dies. Where two or more authors have collaborated on a work, copyright extends for fifty years after the death of the longest-living author, and in the case of a work published anonymously or under a pen-name, copyright lasts for fifty years after publication. Once the appropriate period has passed, the work passes into the public domain, and can be freely used by anybody.

The copyright protection afforded to New Zealand writers is theoretically valid overseas as well, but this is obviously difficult to monitor or enforce. For this reason, the Berne Union and the Universal Copyright Convention were brought into existence. Upon joining, each member state agrees to give the works of writers from other member states the same protection it gives its own. In short, the conditions that need to be fulfilled for protection are that each work must contain the © symbol, the name of the copyright owner and the first year of publication.

The Berne Union includes Britain, the majority of Commonwealth countries and most European nations. The United States, the Soviet Union and most of South America are signatories to the Universal Copyright Convention, with several countries being involved in both. The protection that New Zealand writers receive in these countries corresponds more or less to that at home, with one or two variations.

Until very recently, many Asian countries were notorious for ignoring copyright conventions. Some of the major offenders, such as the People's Republic of China and Taiwan, have now joined international copyright treaties. Significant improvements in protection policies worldwide are now expected for writers.

Breach of copyright

Breach of copyright may occur in four ways: reproduction, adaptation, publication or performance. Reproduction of a whole work, or a substantial part of it, in a magazine or newspaper may constitute a breach of copyright. Unauthorised adaptation such as translation or adaptation for the screen or stage also falls into this category. Publication of an entire work still under copyright would obviously fall foul of the law, and unauthorised performance of a literary work, e.g., drama or poetry readings, can also be deemed an infringement.

There are a number of exceptions to these situations. Schools, universities and libraries are exempt under certain circumstances; there is also provision for work to be quoted extensively, or reproduced, for research and private study. Works can be used for purposes of criticism and review, and also whilst reporting current events. The Crown may use material without first consulting the owner of copyright, but this rarely, if ever, occurs in New Zealand. In all cases, a full acknowledgement of the source of the work is expected.

Photocopying

Copyright Licensing Limited (CLL) is a company set up after a detailed investigation by the Book Publishers' Association into copyright matters, with a view to controlling mechanical copying by third parties. As in schemes operating in Britain, Australia and the United States, the company licenses regular copiers and collects a fee from them when material is reproduced. Authors get a percentage of the fees collected, according to an agreement between themselves, their publishing company and Copyright Licensing Limited. Ask your publisher for further details, or contact Copyright Licensing Limited or the Book Publishers' Association of New Zealand, both at P.O. Box 36477, Northcote, Auckland, email cll@copyright.co.nz and bpanz@copyright.co.nz respectively.

Using copyright material

The most common situation in which you will need to get permission to use copyright material occurs when you want to use it as part of your own work, perhaps quoting a poem, or using sections of another text to illustrate a point. It is difficult to tell exactly when the amount of material used becomes 'substantial', but as a general guide a maximum of forty to fifty words is regarded as acceptable.

Ascertaining the ownership of copyright may be difficult sometimes, but usually an approach to a book's publisher or directly to the author will bring results. A request for permission to use copyright material should be accompanied with an explanation of why you wish to use it, where it will be used and how widely it will be distributed. Most major publishing houses have a permissions editor to deal with such requests and to whom letters should be addressed. If you are working to a deadline, allow plenty of time for a reply, and mention your deadline in your letter.

Some authors or publishers will ask a small fee for copyright permission. This is not usually prohibitive, and is often waived. A full acknowledgement of the copyright work is always expected and some publishers or authors may ask for this to be in a specific form. Always oblige. Obtaining permission to use lyrics in a work may prove more difficult, and a request for payment is more common.

Needless to say, all correspondence concerning the use of copyright material should be kept, in case of dispute.

Defamation

Broadly speaking, defamation can be described as an attack on somebody's good reputation; its original meaning was 'to spread evil reports'. Libel, a false statement that damages a person's reputation, comes under this category, as do statements which may 'lower the plaintiff in the estimation of right-thinking members of society', statements which deliberately set out to damage someone's reputation through 'hatred, contempt or ridicule', and statements which tend to make people 'shun and avoid' the defamed person.

When can defamation occur?

With a little care and attention to detail, it is usually possible to avoid making libellous statements; the other three cases can be a little more tricky. Defamatory statements may include insinuations of improper or criminal conduct, incompetency, bankruptcy or even ridicule.

In addition, any untrue statement about a political candidate (before polling day) or a statement likely to influence voters may be defamatory; so too are remarks expressing the view that people are not 'properly' married or that their children are illegitimate.

On top of all this, defamation can occur even if you didn't mean it to, or if the words you used can be construed to mean something which is not stated. Repeating someone else's story is no defence either, and publishers and owners of publications may also be liable to legal action.

Defence

You will, of course, want to exercise your own judgement about the material you intend to use, rather than get to the point where a court decides. If it does reach that unfortunate stage, however, there are several defences against a defamation action.

The first is 'privilege', i.e., a statement made under special circumstances, such as in court. 'Fair comment' may need a good lawyer to prove, and is acceptable only if it is based on facts. The plaintiff doesn't need to prove the defamatory remarks were untrue; but if the defendant can prove them to be true, 'justification' may be a defence. If the 'consent' of the defamed person was obtained before the remarks were published, this also is a defence.

Settlement out of court may be an option and, in some situations, an apology might work. The best policy is to try to avoid having to use any of these defences. If a work is contentious in any way it is better to seek legal advice before publication.

Legal advice

In New Zealand, the legal profession has few members who specialise in the areas where writers may have problems. You should always consult your own lawyer first, where a dispute has arisen; he or she may be able to offer advice or refer you to an appropriate solicitor. You can also contact the New Zealand Law Society for information about lawyers who do specialise in this aspect of the law.

The New Zealand Society of Authors has a legal advice committee that exists to help members with any problems, in particular with matters concerning copyright and contracts. In some cases, NZSA members may be offered subsidised legal help. Members should, in the first instance, contact the executive director at the NZSA, P.O. Box 67013, Mt Eden, Auckland 1349. Tel & Fax (09) 379 4801. Email nzsa@clear.net.nz.

A definitive guide to New Zealand law and how it relates to writers is *Media Law in New Zealand* by J. Burrows and U. Cheer, published by Oxford University Press. In addition, *New Zealand Intellectual Property Reports* edited by A. Brown, published by Butterworths, provides considerable information on copyright and copyright protection.

11 New Zealand Taxation

Death and taxes are certainties, as the well-known saying goes. However, the circumstances of both vary enormously according to the individual. The notes below act only as a general guide to New Zealand taxation as it applies to writers; for full details you should contact your nearest Inland Revenue office. The New Zealand Society of Authors also has a handy publication entitled *Writers and Tax* by Kathleen Gallagher. Updated annually, it is available for $7 (members) and $12 (non-members), p&p inclusive. Send a cheque and self-addressed label to NZSA, PO Box 67013, Mt Eden, Auckland 1349.

You pay income tax on the net profit from your business (writing) — that's all the income that comes in, minus allowable business expenses.

Provisional tax

The tax you pay on any income that does not have tax deducted at its source is called provisional tax. This includes business income, if you are self-employed (full or part-time), and royalties. If your residual income tax on income from writing is $2,500 or more, after deducting any tax credits for which you're eligible, then you must pay provisional tax.

Provisional tax is due in three instalments during the year. The amount is based on your income from business and royalties in the previous year. If your net writing income and royalties after expenses was less than approximately $10,000, then you may not have to pay provisional tax, depending on any other income you may have and your marginal rate of tax. You can make voluntary payments, however (although you may end up having to pay later, anyway). The ways of calculating your provisional tax payments, if you have earned more than that amount, are outlined in the Inland Revenue's booklet IR289, Provisional Tax. This booklet can be downloaded from www.ird.govt.nz.

Expenses

Most expenses that are part of the cost of running your business are tax deductible, except for the cost of buying capital assets. You can claim legitimate expenses from your business (i.e. writing). These include: Accident Compensation premiums, less salaries and wages paid to people who work for you, rent, rates, stationery, accountant's fees, travelling expenses and other more specific expenses. You may also claim a proportion of home expenses, e.g. mortgage interest, if you work from home.

You can claim depreciation on the cost of the capital assets, to allow for their decline in value. Depreciation allowances for the various pieces of equipment you might use in your writing are outlined in the IR260 pamphlet Depreciation.

Accounts recording both income and expenditure must be kept to qualify for these expenses. Your accounts should include bank statements, invoices, receipts, and any other material to support your claims. If your car is used to assist your writing, you must keep a log-book for at least three months every three years. You will need to record the distance travelled on each project, the reason for the trip and the total distance travelled each year on both business and non-business.

The use of a tax consultant or accountant can be well worth investigating — their advice and know-how can more than recoup the cost of their fees (which, in any case, are also tax deductible).

Accident compensation

Self-employed people must pay ACC premiums to ACC and a Residual Claims levy to the Inland Revenue each year. The amount of the premiums is based on the income you received from your writing and royalties in the previous year, and is tax deductible. The rates of the premiums are determined according to the nature of your work. For more help you may find helpful the ACC's Self-Employed Premiums booklet.

Goods and Services Tax

If you earn more than $40,000 a year gross from your writing activities you must register for GST. You may voluntarily register if your income is less than $40,000. What this means is that, simply, you are able to recoup the GST that you pay on everything you purchase in the pursuit of your business. You must, of course, also charge your customers and clients GST. Being GST registered adds a certain amount of book-keeping to your responsibilities, but it can be worth it if you are serious about earning a living from writing. The Inland Revenue Department will be able to advise you how to go about getting registered for GST. In most cases, you will have to provide a detailed claim for any GST refund every two or six months, depending on your system. If you are in the league of earning substantial amounts from writing, you are strongly advised to think about retaining an accountant to oversee your financial procedures. This person will also be able to fill you in on the finer details of this tax. Some accountancy firms offer free seminars for small businesses explaining their taxation responsibilities. It may be worth finding out if there are any such seminars in your area, or if a reputable firm of accountants will advise you (at a reasonable cost) as to procedures you should be following.

Alternatively, there are several good books that deal with this and other aspects of small business and small business book-keeping. For example, the Smart Business Guide IR320 gives an overview of your record keeping responsibilities with the Inland Revenue Department. Ensure you consult up-to-date editions, as taxation laws and levels are subject to change each year. Also available is the Inland Revenue's booklet IR375 GST Guide which has full details on GST obligations.

The Inland Revenue Department

If you have any queries about your tax situation you are strongly advised to contact the Inland Revenue Department — it is there to help you complete your tax obligations competently and fairly. ALWAYS be honest, declare all money you receive; odds are that the person you received it from will claim it as an expense and it will be traced to you. Keep yourself in the Inland Revenue's good books and you'll have no problems.

12 Publish Yourself

As desktop publishing systems become more and more accessible to the everyday user — in terms of both cost and usability — there are now, more than ever, opportunities for writers to publish their own work successfully. While it's possible, however, you should consider very carefully if this is the way you want to proceed. Design and layout, and the printing itself, can be expensive, and marketing the finished product also presents difficulties. Like any business venture, self-publishing should be carefully planned before you start to spend money. Prepare yourself a business plan, with full estimates of costs and returns — and be realistic in your expectations! Who exactly are you going to sell to — and how? Who is your target audience? What sort of promotion and marketing are you going to have to do? Are you going to have time to travel around all the outlets you think might be interested — or should you appoint an agent or distributor to handle this side of publishing? Will you consider e-publishing? What publicity can you gain for your book through reviews, or press releases, or advertising, or creating your own website? Do your research and make your choices BEFORE you have a garage full of books!

Before you head off to the printer or set about creating a website, it is a good idea to sit and think through your real reasons for self-publishing. If you have had a manuscript rejected by a number of publishers, this does not necessarily mean that commercial publishers cannot see the potential of your work — it might mean that, having done their market research, they simply feel there is little or no market for it. Do you want to risk taking the costs of publishing your work on your own shoulders in that case? Also, hard though it may be to accept, publishers may have simply felt that your work was not of a publishable standard. Be honest with yourself.

Assuming you are going to proceed, there are a number of steps you will need to go through to get your book out to your readers. These are outlined below.

Editorial

The author is almost always not the best person to perform editorial work on a manuscript. As they say, two heads are better than one, and you may be so 'close' to your manuscript that you cannot spot possible errors, or changes of emphasis, or even basic typing mistakes that could detract from the final product. Ask someone else to have a close look at your work. They may be able to make some very sensible suggestions on improving the text. An experienced editor will also pay close attention to matters such as consistency of style, grammar, and punctuation. Set yourself a 'style' and follow it religiously. Nothing looks more amateur than a text that is a mixture of styles and punctuation usage. You may not notice it, but it is guaranteed to irritate your readers as they struggle through your work!

Design and format

Assuming you have decided to publish your book in the traditional manner — i.e., a printed book — you will need to consider the following questions. How do you want your finished product to look? What size will it be? How will the text sit on the page? Will it be illustrated and, if so, to what extent? You must sit down at a very early stage and spend time thinking about every aspect of your publication, because changing your ideas during the process can be expensive and frustrating for all involved.

Once you have settled on a basic format, it is a good idea to establish a template showing your preferred layout for prelims (title page, contents, acknowledgements, introduction etc.) and the body of the text, as well as any endmatter (appendices, index and so on) using word-processing software (Microsoft Word etc.) or a graphic design package. Leave enough space at the top and bottom of the page, too, to enable you to add page numbers (folios) and header and footer text where necessary.

At this early design stage, you should also indicate – and highlight clearly on the manuscript – your choice of typeface (font) and size (point size) for chapter headings, subheadings and body text.

Print out sample pages so you can get some idea of what the finished book will look like. If you choose an 'average' page for sample setting, this will also give you a guide to the probable length (extent)of your book. When calculating page numbers, don't forget to add in title pages, indexes, tables of contents and so on. At this stage you should also estimate the number and size of illustrations, as these will have an impact on your final number of pages.

Quotations

Having established your parameters for production, you are now in a position to start getting estimates for the jobs you are either unable to do or don't want to do yourself. These jobs will usually encompass:

- typesetting and design
- illustration processing
- printing.

Typesetting and design

Before you pass your manuscript to the typesetter or designer, you need to ensure the document is formatted in a way they can use. Their software (which will most likely be a design package such as Indesign or Quark) is likely to be different from what you are running on your PC or notebook. When getting quotes, establish what file format you need to provide and what formatting styles will transfer into a design program and what needs to be stripped out. Printers now often print straight from digital files and if you are confident of your design skills and have the necessary software, you can look after this stage yourself. You will need to liaise with the printer at an early stage to ensure you know how the file needs to be prepared for print. In general, however, make sure that what is on the disk is exactly as you want it to be on the page. Small changes can be made at the first proof stage, but once your book goes to film for printing, changes become very expensive.

Ask for written quotations, and choose the production company or printer you feel most comfortable with. They may be able to offer you tips on text design as well. Listen to them — they are likely to be more experienced than you! Once you have decided who will produce your book, ensure you provide them with full, clear instructions on how you want your text to appear.

Illustration processing

Just as there are many different kinds of illustrations – line drawings, graphs, charts, black and white photographs (half tones), colour photographs, prints, transparencies and digital files – there is also a variety of reproduction methods available. Your particular requirements, and the form in which you supply the material to your production company, will need to be discussed with them beforehand. You may wish to use the services of a graphic designer, or if you have software like Photoshop available you may be able to do much of the preparatory work.

Remember, however, that when you supply digital images, the resolution must be 300 dpi – or better – at the size you wish to reproduce the image. Diagrams, charts or line drawings you may be able to digitise by scanner and incorporate into your document on disk. If the illustrations are digitised you can manipulate the size and crop them as you wish on your computer – again, Photoshop or another graphic manipulation program would be useful in this case.

If your illustrations are being supplied for the designer or printer to scan, instructions need to be given for enlarging or reducing them. Make sure your sizings and croppings are correct. Ensure that any 'pre-press' scanning or image processing and image manipulation is included in your quote.

Printing

To get an accurate quotation from a printer, you will need to provide them with very detailed specifications for printing. (A sample specification is given on page 79.)

There are several points to note in the sample specification. You will first need to decide on the thickness of paper you want to use. Most printers will be happy to show you the kinds of paper they normally stock, and you can make a decision on those. Most papers are categorised by weight — 'gsm', or grams per square metre. Ask to see a printed sample of the paper you are considering so you can check the amount of 'show through' from one side of the printed paper to the other. It is best to stick with standard sizes for trim size (the size they will cut your folded and bound book to).

Binding costs can vary a lot, depending on the type you use. Saddle stitched (or stapled) is easily the cheapest. Perfect bound refers to pages that are cut or perforated and then glued into a spine.

Your colour specifications should be carefully stated. In the specification example, 2/2 means two ink colours are to be used on each side of the page; 2/1 would mean two colours on one side of a page, only one on the other. If you want to use another colour besides black, you should use the PMS colour matching system. Basically, this is a collection of number codes that correspond to certain standard colours. PMS colour charts are available at most graphic arts suppliers, or your printer or typesetter may be able to advise you on accurate codings.

Once you have finalised your layout and design (including the cover) and assembled all your images, illustrations etc., pass them on to your printer or book production company with a covering letter clearly restating all your specifications. Don't leave anything to chance — printers are always grateful for too much information, rather than too little.

Proofs

Your printer will provide you with proofs. These will be exactly what you get in the finished book — if you don't make any amendments at this stage. The proofs should be examined in minute detail, and every error, inkspot or amendment you wish to make at this stage must be marked clearly with instructions as to what you want done. Your printer will probably want you to sign an approval sheet to confirm you have checked the proofs and are happy with what you see. If you are not, ask for your corrections to be made and another proof supplied.

The finished product and how to get rid of it

Once the printer has your approval, they will start printing and binding. When everything is finished, your book will be despatched to you, and the hard part begins — selling it to potential readers! Promoting your book will take as long as, if not longer than, it took to write it and have it printed. You need a carefully thought-out marketing plan, that includes strategies

23 January 2007
SPECIFICATION FOR QUOTATION

TITLE: My Brilliant Career, by Mitchell Smith

EXTENT: 64 pages + cover.

PAPER:
Cover 300 gsm matt art (or nearest stock)
Text 140 gsm matt art (or nearest stock)
When quoting, please submit samples of proposed paper stocks at size specified below.

TRIM SIZE: A5 105 x 148.5 mm portrait

BINDING:
Please quote on 2 options:
Option A – Saddle Stitch Option B – Perfect Bound

COLOUR:
Outside front and rear cover 2C Black + 1 PMS colour
Inside front and rear cover 1C (black)
Text 2/2C Black + 1 PMS colour per book

ARTWORK:
Black text supplied on disk, PC-compatible, Microsoft Word Vista (or please advise format requirements)
Other artwork, supplied as approximately 20 halftones

QUANTITIES:
Please quote on:
(a) 500 copies (b) 1000 copies

SCHEDULE:
Please provide a working schedule for production, and an estimated date for despatch, assuming:
– artwork delivered to you on 31 September 2007
– one week approval from receipt of proofs by me

DESPATCH:
Please include charge for despatch of finished books to my address.

PAYMENT:
Payment 60 days from date of despatch.

Quotations required by 30 April 2007.
If further details are required, please contact the undersigned.

Mitchell Smith

for selling to bookshops and libraries, through direct mail campaigns, and perhaps online through a website.

Promoting your book

There are several techniques you can explore and utilise for creating awareness of your book. Send letters to prospective booksellers, outlining the book's title and selling price, and include your name and contact details. Send as many review copies as you can afford to magazines and newspapers (but don't expect them back). Phone your local radio station and community newspaper and ask if there is the possibility of any free advertising. Exercise caution about buying advertising space — even a few centimetres in a single column can set you back several hundred dollars, and you'll rarely recover costs such as this. Write down all the various organisations and community groups that may be interested in your book, and send them a promotional letter that includes an offer if they order a copy (e.g. 10 per cent off the selling price, plus free delivery). Some publications have regular book giveaways and this can be an effective means of getting exposure for your book in exchange for a couple of free copies.

www.mybestseller.co.nz

Your very own website can be an extremely useful and cost-effective marketing tool. It allows a self-publisher to promote their book internationally, 24 hours a day, seven days a week. A carefully crafted and well-designed website can incorporate advertising material, a colour photograph of the book cover, reviews from the media, and in some cases a system that allows for orders to be placed. However, they come at a price. The initial costs of setting up a website are high — unless you have the technical expertise, design flair, and creativity to build your own site, you'll need to invest in the services of a professional website designer, which can cost thousands of dollars. Website creation software programs are available (such as Microsoft FrontPage) that convert your straightforward document into an all-singing, all-dancing website. The major ISPs also provide website creation solutions for very affordable fees.

Whether you do it yourself or pay someone else to do it, you will have to plan the site carefully beforehand and write the copy — something you, as a writer, should be good at already. The more effort you put into the planning stages, the better the finished product will be. As with any marketing campaign, you need to identify your target market and be clear about what you want your website to achieve. Will it simply advertise your book? Will it feature reviews and other promotional material? Will you include a photograph of the cover and perhaps one of yourself? Will it function as a sales outlet? How will prospective buyers contact you?

Once you've got your site planned out and typed up, you're ready to contact your ISP to have the site published. Your ISP will store your site for you on their server, and the web address for your site will become something like www.xtra.co.nz/mybestseller. This can be something of a mouthful for customers to remember, so some writers take the next step and invest in their own domain name. A domain name is your unique identity on the Internet. It provides you with a way to communicate with your customers using a name that is personalised to you, such as www.mybestseller.co.nz. The domain name system is administered internationally in the USA by the Internet Assigned Numbers Authority (IANA). IANA delegates responsibility for administering domain name space on a regional basis. The '.nz' domain name space is administered by ISOCNZ (the Internet Society of New Zealand Inc.) through its subsidiary, the New Zealand Internet Registry Ltd. This company trades under the name of Domainz. Domainz fees are levied annually and are payable in advance. In the first year, the basic fee package for a new domain name holder (rather like a post office box holder) is $61.87 including GST. Visit the Domainz website for more information at www.domainz.net.nz or call 0800 366 2469. Domainz offer a range of solutions for helping you to get started online, including website design, registration, web hosting fees and search engine submissions.

When you register a domain name it belongs exclusively to you, and prevents other companies from using it (assuming you have the right to the name). With a domain name you can have several different email addresses, such as joebloggs@mybestseller.co.nz; you can also receive emails for info@mybestseller.co.nz or sales@mybestseller.co.nz.

Of course, once you have your own web presence, you can't just sit back and wait for the orders to pour in. You need to let people know that your website exists, and once again your old-fashioned marketing techniques come in handy. Include your email and website addresses in all your correspondence. Contact the various search engines and register your website with them. Refer potential customers to your website. Make sure it stays attractive by updating it regularly with fresh reviews and your forthcoming titles!

Selling to the trade

If you intend to sell to bookshops (and chances are you will inevitably get orders at some stage from at least your local bookseller, especially if your book is about local history or a local celebrity), you will need to work out your costings beforehand so that you can negotiate trade discounts. Independent booksellers will want at least 33 or 35 per cent discount off the selling price; the major chains will require 40 or even 50 per cent. You should estimate how much you'll need to cover promotion costs and distribution (postage, packaging, etc.), and you should know how much each book will have cost to produce. Don't forget to build in your own profit (after all, this is a business venture).

To get an idea of the eventual selling price, multiply your unit production cost by five. This will allow you to negotiate trade discounts, cover your production and promotion costs, have enough to pay the GST, and make a tidy profit at the end (assuming that you manage to sell them all).

Do not expect trade customers to pay the costs of sending their orders to them. Be clear with clients when you accept orders. Your terms should be free of postage and packing, providing that booksellers order a number of copies. Consider reducing your trade discount for single-copy orders. Some booksellers may suggest that you supply them on a sale-or-return basis, which means that they only pay you for the copies that they sell, and any left over are returned to you at a future date (often well below mint condition and therefore unsellable). Agreeing to supply a bookseller on sale or return may be the only way in which you can get your book onto their shelves, but it's a practice that is best avoided by self-publishers.

Expect to have your invoices paid by the 20th of the following month. Keep a careful record of the booksellers that have taken copies of your book, the quantity they took, and the terms of agreement. Keep in touch with individual booksellers (preferably with the main book buyer rather than the counter staff); offer to restock their shelves for them if they run out, rather than wait for their reordering system to catch up with sales.

E-publishing and e-books

One of the downsides of traditional publishing is that many books never make it to the bookshop. Authors struggle to get their work published because traditional publishing is a matter of economics. A printed book is an expensive commodity to produce in small numbers, therefore commercial publishers will only accept a book if they think they can make a profit from it — which means (in New Zealand terms) selling a few thousand copies. Because of the size of the New Zealand market, it is difficult to get particular types of books published, such as romantic fiction, thrillers, and fantasy novels.

With affordable computers and the Internet widely available, virtually anyone can self-publish their literary work. Converting your novel into a website is a simple, if somewhat crude, way of self-publishing your masterpiece but makes it instantly available at a fraction of the cost of traditional publishing to hundreds of millions of potential readers. However, it is difficult to read a large novel off a computer screen. Until recently, one of the major hurdles to the commercial viability of electronic publishing, or 'e-publishing', was the readability factor. People still prefer to read from a small portable device (i.e., a book).

With the development of some revolutionary advanced technology, commercial electronic publishing has been made a reality. Electronic books (or 'e-books') are revolutionising the traditional publishing world.

E-books

An e-book is a digital book that you can read on a computer screen or on an electronic device such as a Palm or other handheld computer. Dedicated e-book reading devices, such as the eBookman, are also available but are expensive, dependent on batteries for portability, and don't like being dropped; the range of titles available for them is limited to a selected list. E-books are available in every category and genre, from bestsellers to classic works. They are very inexpensive to produce and there are virtually no distribution costs. The contents can be updated or changed in an instant — very useful if your book is particularly topical. E-books are available online, and can be delivered in a number of different formats. They can be downloaded from the Internet and printed, downloaded into an electronic reading device, or downloaded and stored on disk. You can buy and download as many e-books as you like at any one time, and store them indefinitely on your computer as an e-book library.

Before downloading an e-book and being able to read it, you must first install the appropriate reader software, such as Microsoft Reader or Adobe Acrobat eBook Reader. Both of these are free and can be downloaded from the major e-book websites, such as Amazon (www.amazon.com) and Barnes & Noble (www.ebooks.barnesandnoble.com).

The length of time needed to download a file depends on the size of the e-book and the speed of your computer's modem.

Microsoft Reader software features ClearType display technology, which makes text appear crisp and clear on LCD screens and includes such features as integrated dictionary support and electronic annotations. The Acrobat eBook Reader allows you to 'sharpen' the text so that it is easier on the eye. Both Microsoft and Adobe readers have built-in security and encryption features to protect against copyright violations, which means you cannot copy an e-book and email it to a friend.

Converting your Word document into an e-book

The first thing to do is decide which software product you'll use to package your e-book. One of the major choices of e-book publishers is Adobe Acrobat (visit their website at www.adobe.com). Acrobat formats your e-book so that it fits perfectly on the customer's screen, and Acrobat-created documents are accessible to customers with both PCs and Macintosh computers (you don't want to limit your market). Another option is to create your e-book as an HTML file (HTML, or hypertext mark-up language, is the same language used to make web pages). This method gives you the opportunity to make your e-book a multimedia production, with animation, audio, and video clips included. Once it's created, you need to make your e-book 'download ready', meaning that it will have to be compressed so that it downloads quickly onto the customer's computer. WinZip (www.winzip.com) is a popular compression program that makes this task very easy. Lastly, you will have to 'upload' your e-book to your web server. Your ISP will provide details and assistance in doing this.

Commercial e-publishers

If you're not up to the task of creating your own e-book, you could try contacting an electronic publishing house. There are a number of dedicated e-publishers who only publish e-books, not print-and-bound books (enter 'e-publishing' into one of the web's search engines), and increasingly the major traditional publishers are setting up their own e-publishing divisions.

Commercial e-publishers operate much like commercial print publishers — they publish, sell, and distribute e-books. Authors submit their text electronically to an editor who decides whether it's marketable and/or appropriate for the e-publisher's list. If it is accepted, the work is edited, proofread, then published and promoted on the e-publisher's website.

The major difference between traditional publishing and e-publishing is the way in which authors are paid for their work. Traditional publishers will offer a royalty of around 10 per cent of the selling price, or — if you're lucky — you may be able to negotiate a lump sum paid up front as an advance against the anticipated sales of the book. Commercial e-publishers, on the other hand, share in the actual royalties received with the author — anywhere from 20 per cent to 70 per cent, with a standard rate of around 40 per cent. Royalty rates vary considerably from one e-publisher to another, so contracts should be read carefully for details of payment, the length of the contract, and the exact rights being purchased by the e-publisher (some demand exclusive electronic rights).

Another option is to offer your book to an online bookseller. Amazon.com pioneered this arena with their Advantage program for authors, but other sites such as barnesandnoble.com also offer programs for the self-publisher.

Print on demand

Print on demand, or POD, is a technology that allows for the printing of small quantities of paperback books. Many e-publishers can provide a POD service, which involves storing your book in digital format, then printing and binding that book only when you place an order for it. Design and graphics services are offered for an additional fee to give an eye-catching, professional look to the book. The downside of POD is that it is quite expensive and that most bookstores and libraries do not accept POD books. One aspect of POD technology that is causing a stir in the publishing world is that, once converted to a digital format, a book will never technically be out of print.

Blogging

Short for web log, blogging has had a huge impact on communications in recent years and has shaken up traditional journalism. A blog is basically an on-line journal, diary or newsletter that is frequently updated and when successful establishes a regular readership. There are millions of active blogs — some are based on personal observations, follow a theme, specific subject or area of interest, while others deal with news-based subject matter and explore controversial issues. All are written in a style that reflects the personality of the writer, or the website associated with the blog. Many offer readers the opportunity to comment on what has been written and links to other like-minded blogs.

Some blogs are written by established journalists, many more are by amateur writers. Starting a blog is very simple – all you basically need is an Internet connection. There are a range of blogging sites and the first step is to find one which appeals to you. Use a search engine such as Google to look at the different providers, such as www.blogger.com or www.Livejournal.com

Setting up a blog requires no specific technical know-how. Most sites offer a variety of templates to choose from — select the colours, column layout and overall look that you want and once you've signed up you can personalise your site further, including your name, interests, images, etc.

The key to a popular blog is to update it regularly — the most successful ones feature short regular updates (at least once a day) which are either full of personal observation or controversial information and opinions. Some blogs are devoted to a particular hobby or pursuit with readers sharing and swapping hints and advice.

Sites such as GoogleAdSense and AmazonAssocID allow bloggers with an established readership the opportunity to make money by placing ads on their blogs. Before you start counting the dollars though, it's worth noting that there is huge competition for 'hits' — people visiting your blog online to read it. However, blogs can be used as a way of assessing general interest in specific subjects or themes.

Offline blogging clients, such as BlogJet or ecto, offer word processing systems for blogging which allow you to write when not online, and then upload your post when you connect to the Internet.

Sources of assistance

Self-Publishers' Association of New Zealand

P.O. Box 27546, Auckland. Tel (09) 527 1287

Email self_publishers_nz@hotmail.com Website www.self-publishers.org.nz

The Self-Publishers' Association is a support organisation for writers who have self-published or are planning to publish, their own work. It focuses on the nuts and bolts of how to self-publish and will post members' book promotions on its website.

New Zealand Society of Authors

P.O. Box 67013, Mt Eden, Auckland 1349. Tel & Fax (09) 379 9801

Email nzsa@clear.net.nz

The NZSA cannot undertake to find publishers or booksellers for your work, and does not engage in publishing collections of writers' work. Instead if offers suggestions on how to research likely publishers for your work, and has a number of useful booklets that are available to members and non-members. These include: *Marketing Your Book* by Joan Rosier-Jones ($15 members, $20 non-members, p&p inclusive), which discusses how to work with your publisher, or how to handle it yourself; *Electronic Publishing* by Tim Jones ($7 members, $12 non-members, p&p inclusive), a look at e-books, POD technology, e-zines (online magazines), and the advantages and disadvantages of publishing on the web; and *Self-publish: A Writer's Guide* ($15 members, $20 non-members).

13 Metropolitan and Daily Newspapers

All the metropolitan and daily newspapers carry national and international news. Often this is supplied by the New Zealand Press Association (NZPA), Reuters or other agencies. In the cases of smaller regional newspapers it is sometimes relayed from other newspapers in major centres. Larger newspapers will also sometimes lift features or pieces of special interest out of overseas newspapers. The following outlines focus on areas in which features and small news stories written by freelance writers could be successful. In most cases, articles of a local or regional flavour are called for. General articles about lifestyles, leisure pursuits, personality profiles, travel, etc., are also widely used.

Overall, newspapers are not a particularly lucrative market for the freelance writer in New Zealand, unless you are a 'name' writer. Nevertheless, making yourself known to the editors and features editors of newspapers can sometimes bring in commissions and other work. Payments for feature articles from outside vary enormously, and there are often no set rates for editorial contributions. The editor assesses your submission, and depending on a number of criteria, such as length, topicality, etc., decides what it is worth. Although payment may be small (or, in some cases, non-existent), publication alone can often be rewarding — and lead to more work.

Notwithstanding the above, the number of newspapers published in New Zealand, when the local community newspapers are included, is enormous, and there is plenty of scope for the enterprising freelancer. Take time to study the newspaper for which you would like to write — analyse its content, page layout and format, and do this on a regular basis. Study the adverts — advertisers pay big money to sell their wares and will have gone to some lengths to determine the newspaper's target market. Remember that newspapers are a dynamic form of media, and the fresh approach of a new writer may be just what the editor is seeking at a particular time.

Note: some newspapers can be slow to reply to freelance contributions, and sometimes they will not acknowledge your submission at all. This is something which happens because of the pressures and time considerations under which an editor often works. Don't regard this as a discourtesy (even though it sometimes is), and don't be hesitant about ringing up an editor and asking what has happened to your article, either, after a reasonable time period. Be aware that contributions of a general nature are often held for some time, until a space can be found for them. Keep a copy of any articles that have been submitted, with the date on which you sent them in and the name of any editor you spoke to.

Try to look ahead — think about what will be breaking news tomorrow, next week, next month: it may become the basis of an article that will be accepted. Often newspapers will plan many weeks ahead for special advertising features centred around a trade or activity, such as house renovation, or holiday destinations, or other general consumer topics.

If you have established a good relationship with the features editor, you may be able to enquire from time to time if any such specials are coming up — perhaps you could submit some material for consideration to them.

Useful websites:
Newspaper Press Association of NZ (Inc): www.nzpa.co.nz
NZ Press Council: www.presscouncil.org.nz
Fairfax Media: www.fairfax.co.nz
APN News and Media: www.apn.com.au

Ashburton Guardian
P.O. Box 77, Ashburton. Tel (03) 307 7900 Fax (03) 307 7980
Email enquiries@theguardian.co.nz
Website www.ashburton.co.nz and www.ashburtonguardian.co.nz
The *Ashburton Guardian* is a daily paper that runs regular features in the areas of women's interests, lifestyle, sport, racing, money matters, gardening, motoring and farming. It also has a regular children's page. The paper is interested in feature articles of relevance to readers in the Ashburton district, such as profiles of notable or interesting people and places. A preliminary letter to the editor is always advisable. Black and white and colour photographs are used.

Bay of Plenty Times
Private Bag 12002, Tauranga.
Tel (07) 577 7770 Fax (07) 578 0047
Email editor@bopp.co.nz
Website www.bayofplentytimes.co.nz
The *Bay of Plenty Times* is a daily and serves the whole of the Bay of Plenty. In the paper, there are articles on women's interests, gardening, travel, cars, finance and topical material of interest to the rural sector. Book reviews are also published. The newspaper may be interested in articles of interest to local people, such as profiles or matters of community concern. Black and white, or colour photographs may be submitted, although they are not necessary. Payment is by arrangement and varies according to the content

of the article. Contact should be made initially with the chief reporter or editor via phone, fax or email.

Taranaki Daily News
P.O. Box 444, New Plymouth. Tel (06) 759 0880 Fax (06) 758 4653
Email jonathan.mackenzie@tnl.co.nz
Website www.fairfaxnz.co.nz
Taranaki's only daily paper, and one of the largest provincial morning newspapers, the *Daily News* reflects New Plymouth's status as a city within a rural area. Articles on lifestyle and fashion go side by side with features on rural matters, agricultural innovations and occasionally local history. Freelance contributions are used occasionally. Pieces with local content are generally used. The preferred length is approximately 1000 words for features, and a preliminary letter to the editor is appreciated. Black and white prints and colour transparencies are welcomed when accompanying articles. All articles accepted are paid for. The amount paid depends on the editor's assessment of the merit of each piece.

The Daily Post
P.O. Box 1442, Rotorua.
Tel (07) 348 6199 Fax (07) 348 0220
Email news@dailypost.co.nz
Website www.dailypost.co.nz
The Rotorua daily newspaper serves a wide regional area around the Rotorua district. It has several regular areas of interest. These include finance, news of farming developments, items on industrial matters (forestry is a large industry in this region) and computers. More general features cover women's interests, health, fashion and home improvement ideas. There are regular columns on gardening and dining out. Book reviews and news of events in Rotorua and the surrounding district are also published. *The Daily Post* occasionally accepts freelance articles — payment is by negotiation with the editor. Black and white photographs are welcome.

The Dominion Post
P.O. Box 3740, Wellington. Tel (04) 474 0185 Fax (04) 474 0350
Email editor@dompost.co.nz
Website www.stuff.co.nz
The Dominion Post is published every day except Sunday. It includes such sections as Travel, Long Weekend and Indulgence, which consider submissions from freelancers on a broad range of topics. The method of preferred submission is by email to editor@dompost.co.nz. Payment is by negotiation. Please do not send original illustrations unless requested.

The Ensign
47 Mersey Street, Gore. Tel (03) 208 9280 Fax (03) 208 8949

Email ensign@alliedpress.co.nz
Website www.alliedpress.co.nz
A small daily newspaper focusing on events of interest to readers in Gore and surrounding districts, the *Ensign* rarely uses freelance contributions, but it is always willing to consider suitable articles. Payment is not usually made. If possible photographs should accompany submissions. The *Ensign* regularly features sport, entertainment, books, music, art, gardening, farming and lifestyle stories.

Dannevirke News
P.O. Box 92, Dannevirke.
Tel (06) 374 7081 Fax (06) 374 9353
Dannevirke is the centre of a large farming area, and this daily covers new and events from the nearby rural areas of Hawke's Bay and Manawatu. Features about agricultural and pastoral developments appear regularly, along with other items of interest to farmers and townspeople alike. Articles with a strong local content are considered from freelance writers. Payment, if any, is small and varies according to the nature of the submission. Photographs are always appreciated, and should be in black and white. A preliminary letter to the editor is not essential.

Gisborne Herald
P.O. Box 1143, Gisborne.
Tel (06) 869 0600 Fax (06) 869 0643
Email editorial@gisborneherald.co.nz
Website www.gisborneherald.co.nz
Gisborne's daily paper concentrates on articles with a strong local flavour. It does not use freelance material but will always consider articles of interest to readers in the East Coast area. The paper regularly features material about farming, commerce, lifestyles and sport as well as covering local and international news.

Greymouth Evening Star
P.O. Box 3, Greymouth. Tel (03) 768 7121 Fax (03) 768 6205
Email editor@greystar.co.nz
The *Greymouth Evening Star* provides news to readers throughout Westland, stretching from Westport in the north to Haast in the south, including some of the country's most remote wilderness areas.

Hawke's Bay Today
P.O. Box 180, Hastings. Tel (06) 873 0800 Fax (06) 873 0811
Email editor@hbtoday.co.nz
Website www.hbtoday.co.nz
Hawke's Bay Today, based in Hastings, provides news coverage of the region from Mahia (south of Gisborne) to Dannevirke. A daily paper, *Hawke's Bay*

Today runs regular local, national and human interest features on a wide range of subjects. The editor sometimes accepts freelance contributions in these and other areas of local or regional interest. Payment is variable, depending on the nature and length of the article. A preliminary letter is always advisable before proceeding with any work. *Hawke's Bay Today* prefers contributors to submit colour illustrations with their articles.

Herald on Sunday
P.O. Box 32, Auckland Central. Tel (09) 373 9339 Fax (09) 373 9372
Website www.nzherald.co.nz
A lively mix of current affairs, celebrity news, sports and lifestyle features, with a lift-out colour magazine. It has full-time staff writers and a stable of regular contributors, and communication with the editor is recommended regarding ideas for features or articles.

Horowhenua-Kapiti Chronicle
P.O. Box 547, Levin. Tel (06) 368 5109 Fax (06) 368 5109
The daily Levin newspaper features finance, farming and gardening on its pages, and also provides wide coverage of national and local sport. The paper sometimes uses freelance articles on a range of subjects, and submissions should be marked for the attention of the editor. A preliminary letter is not required. Illustrations for articles (or on their own) are welcomed by the editor. The paper does not, however, usually make payments for articles submitted on speculation.

The Independent
P.O. Box 1409, Auckland. Tel (09) 308 4859 Fax (09) 308 4596
Email news@theindependent.co.nz
Website www.theindependent.co.nz
This national weekly paper takes an in-depth look at political, economic and business affairs within New Zealand, with up-to-date news, stock market information and editorial comment. Most freelance work is commissioned.

Manawatu Evening Standard
P.O. Box 3, Palmerston North. Tel (06) 350 9555
Email editor@msl.co.nz
Website www.manawatustandard.co.nz
The *Manawatu Evening Standard* is published Monday to Friday and services a university city in a predominantly rural area and therefore aside from national and international news, contains a mix of farming and agricultural news and features on campus activities, arts, food, wine and fashion. The paper also features book and theatre reviews and has a regular magazine section appearing weekly.

The features editor welcomes submissions for articles (preferably by email), and will use occasional articles on specialist sports and other specialist features. The paper's format allows for articles of a maximum length of 1000 words to be used, and payment is generally made for articles which are accepted; however it rarely pays for unsolicited contributions. The actual amount of payment varies depending on the length and exclusivity of contributions. A preliminary letter is not always required. Black and white or colour prints should be submitted with articles where possible.

The Marlborough Express
P.O. Box 242, Blenheim. Tel (03) 577 2950 Fax (03) 577 2953
Email editorial@marlexpress.co.nz
Website www.marlexpress.co.nz
Based in Blenheim, *The Marlborough Express* is circulated throughout the Marlborough region, and thus focuses on activities and lifestyles within its area. Regular features include cooking, business, outdoor activities and the arts. The daily edition uses freelance contributions from time to time, especially on topics such as gardening, cooking, politics and comment. A payment may be made for articles used, depending on a number of factors, such as the type of article and the length; the standing of the author also carries some weight. A preliminary letter is not necessary, but samples of work are appreciated if you are considering writing regularly. Feature articles must be submitted at least 48 hours before they are scheduled for print. It is useful to submit colour prints with feature articles.

The *Saturday Express* is put out by the same company, and it concentrates on community news, rather than 'hard news'. A variety of topics of interest to readers in the Marlborough region are examined, and freelance articles are accepted from time to time. Colour prints to accompany any articles are desirable.

National Business Review
P.O. Box 1734, Auckland. Tel (09) 307 1629 Fax (09) 307 5129
Email editor@nbr.co.nz
Website www.nbr.co.nz
The *National Business Review* is a weekly business newspaper published on Fridays. It uses regular contributions from freelance writers, commissioned for their specialist knowledge on a particular aspect of New Zealand business. The paper will consider articles from freelancers who know their subject; the person to approach is the editor. Due to the nature of the *National Business Review*, photographs are not always essential, and where these are submitted they should be in colour. Drawings are sometimes used. Payment is usually made for articles accepted for publication. This varies according to the nature of the article and the qualifications of the writer.

Nelson Mail
P.O. Box 244, Nelson. Tel (03) 548 7079 Fax (03) 546 2549

Email editor@nelsonmail.co.nz
Website www.nelsonmail.co.nz
This paper regularly covers areas such as finance, computers and sport; it also features articles on entertainment, movies and television, the home scene, gardening, health, art and books. It has a weekend magazine section focusing on longer lifestyle pieces. The *Nelson Mail* rarely uses freelance articles, but it is willing to consider anything to which people in the Nelson area can relate. Payment is usually made for articles used, with additional payments for illustrations. Approach the editor first (a preliminary letter is not required, however).

The New Zealand Herald
P.O. Box 32, Auckland. Tel (09) 379 5050 Fax (09) 373 6421
Website www.nzherald.co.nz
Auckland's daily paper (also available online) covers general interest areas in its feature articles — personality profiles, reviews of the theatre, entertainment, the arts, music, lifestyle, fashion, and items of topical interest to Aucklanders. The number of items written by freelancers is low, but the paper is always willing to consider submissions. The newspaper's style and format for writing should be studied carefully before submitting material to the features editor. Payment varies, according to the features editor's assessment. Photographs, in black and white or colour, can accompany articles although they are not essential. A preliminary letter outlining your proposal is always a good idea.

New Zealand Truth
P.O. Box 1327, Auckland. Tel (09) 302 1300 Fax (09) 307 0761
Email editor@truth.co.nz
Website www.fairfaxnz.co.nz
The *Truth* is a weekly newspaper distributed throughout New Zealand, often using freelance writers to work on its stories. The editor prefers professional full-time freelancers rather than those who write for a hobby or pastime, and is always interested in contributions in the following areas: television and entertainment personality profiles, unusual human interest stories (not short stories), articles which examine social issues, and features on lifestyle trends. A preliminary letter is highly advisable — freelance writers work under the editor's instructions. *New Zealand Truth* prefers writers to submit illustrations with their articles — black and white prints, colour prints, transparencies and drawings are all acceptable.

The Northern Advocate
P.O. Box 210, Whangarei. Tel (09) 470 2875 Fax (09) 470 2865
Email editor@northernadvocate.co.nz
Website www.northernadvocate.co.nz
The *Northern Advocate* covers areas such as sport, finance, rural news,

motoring, gardening, personalities, politics, leisure, wine, cooking, the arts and travel. The paper often uses articles on a variety of topics from contributors. The contact person for contributors is the editor. A payment is usually made for articles published. There is no preferred length for articles; this depends entirely on the quality of the writing and the topic. A preliminary letter or email to the editor will usually ascertain if the paper is interested in your ideas. Photographs, either in black and white or colour, should be submitted with material for publication.

The Oamaru Mail
P.O. Box 343, Oamaru. Tel (03) 434 9970 Fax (03) 434 9723
Email daily@oamarumail.co.nz
Articles with local content are considered by the *Oamaru Mail*, although not many freelance articles are used. The *Mail* concentrates on community news and events of relevance to readers in northern Otago; farming, commerce and reviews are also featured in its pages.

Otago Daily Times
P.O. Box 517, Dunedin. Tel (03) 477 4760 Fax (03) 474 7422
Email editor@odt.co.nz
Website www.odt.co.nz
Dunedin's daily newspaper regularly publishes material from a wide range of areas, including home and leisure, travel, cooking and literature. There is also a regular magazine section which has features of all types. The editor prefers articles from freelance contributors to be not more than 1000 words in length, and also to be accompanied by illustrations. These can be in the form of colour (preferable) or black and white prints, or drawings, or emailed images to odtpix@odt.co.nz. A payment is usually made for articles published. This varies according to the news value, the scope of the article, etc. A preliminary letter to the editor is not required, as the *Otago Daily Times* will consider contributions in all areas.

The Press
Private Bag 4722, Christchurch. Tel (03) 364 8464
Email editorial@press.co.nz
Website www.thepress.co.nz
The Press often uses articles from outside contributors, and is willing to consider material relating to anything of interest to its readers in the Canterbury region. Lifestyle, personality profiles, leisure, travel and fitness regularly feature within its pages. There are also frequent articles on books, the arts, music and fashion. Contributions should be addressed to the editor, or appropriate section (for example, arts editor, travel editor, etc). Photographs (in colour or black and white) from freelancers are sometimes used, but are not essential. Payment is always made for articles which appear in *The Press*, but this varies according to the value of the piece.

Southland Times
P.O. Box 805, Invercargill. Tel (03) 211 1130 Fax (03) 218 4349
Email fred.tulett@stl.co.nz
Website www.southlandtimes.co.nz
The *Southland Times* is published each morning except Sunday and covers Southland and Central Otago. The paper has regular columns on women's issues, gardening, motoring, sport, items of interest to farmers, and book reviews. The editor will use articles from freelance writers (generally less than 1000 words) on Southland or Otago themes, and pays for these according to merit. A preliminary letter is not generally required. Black and white or colour prints are acceptable, as well as drawings and illustrations, where suitable. There are no deadlines for feature material — it will be used when appropriate.

Sunday News
P.O. Box 1327, Auckland. Tel (09) 302 1300 Fax (09) 358 3003
Email editor@sunday-news.co.nz
Website www.sundaynews.co.nz
Sunday News is a tabloid paper published nationally and includes lively backgrounds on the latest news, both in New Zealand and overseas, with opinion columns written by some of the country's most outspoken politicians and commentators. The paper includes coverage of the weekend sport and racing, and sports personality profiles are a popular feature. The paper's magazine section is geared towards entertainment, home and lifestyle, and features each week motoring, gardening, recipes, kids' pages, problem pages and horoscopes. Prospective writers should send a preliminary letter to the features editor.

Sunday Star Times
P.O. Box 1327, Auckland 1. Tel (09) 302 1300 Fax (09) 309 0258
Email editor@star-times.co.nz
Website www.sstlive.co.nz
This newspaper has six sections: news, sport, focus, Escape, SUNDAY magazine, Business, About Town (Auckland only) with articles about lifestyle, the arts, film, nostalgia, books, wine, food and entertainment. Payment is usually made for articles which get published; the rate of payment depends on the article and the features editor's assessment of it. Black and white and colour photographs are also sought for illustration, but are not always necessary. A preliminary letter to the relevant features editor is recommended.

Timaru Herald
P.O. Box 46, Timaru. Tel (03) 684 4129 Fax (03) 688 1042
Email dave.wood@timaruherald.co.nz
Website www.timaruherald.co.nz

News from rural areas, sport, business, book reviews and women's interests are regular aspects of the *Timaru Herald*. Freelance contributions in these or other areas of interest to readers in the region are sometimes used by the *Timaru Herald*. A preliminary letter is not essential, but illustrations should be submitted where possible.

Waikato Times
Private Bag 3086, Hamilton. Tel (07) 849 6180 Fax (07) 849 9603
Email editor@waikatotimes.co.nz
Website www.waikatotimes.co.nz
Based in Hamilton, the *Waikato Times* deals with subjects of interest to both its metropolitan and rural readers. There are articles on business, industry and farming. Special features on food, art, drama, books and the home and garden are also used. Outside contributions are sometimes accepted; and a payment is usually made, depending on the article's nature. Articles with a strong local angle generally work best. Photographs and drawings can be considered with submissions.

Wairarapa Times-Age
P.O. Box 445, Masterton. Tel (06) 378 9999 Fax (06) 370 0966
Email office@times-age.co.nz
Website www.times-age.co.nz
Articles about local events, places and personalities will be considered by the *Times-Age*. Although not a large newspaper in circulation terms, the paper occasionally uses material that has been sent in by freelance writers. Farming news and sport feature heavily in the paper, along with news of events and local developments in the Wairarapa; there are also regular sections on music, gardening, home improvements and books. There is a regular children's feature. Illustrations are always welcome; these should be colour or black and white photographs or drawings. A preliminary letter to the editor is preferred.

Wanganui Chronicle
P.O. Box 433, Wanganui. Tel (06) 349 0710 Fax (06) 349 0721
Email news@wanganuichronicle.co.nz
Website www.wanganuichronicle.co.nz
The *Chronicle* features articles about the outdoors, lifestyles, and reviews of the arts, music and entertainment. The newspaper does not use contributions from freelance writers very often, but good stories with a local flavour will be considered. All contributions, with photographs where possible, should be addressed to the editor. Payment is at the editor's discretion.

14 Other Newspapers

Community, or local and suburban, newspapers are one of the fastest growing areas in New Zealand publishing. Virtually every small town, suburb and city has one — their strength and appeal lies in the fact that they service a well-defined area, making them attractive to advertisers. In most cases, they are published from one to three times a week and are generally distributed free to households in their area. The strength of community newspapers can be seen in the fact that many have increased their frequency of publication from once a week or fortnight to two or three times a week in the last few years. Circulation numbers have also boomed.

Community newspapers are a good, if often ignored, market for freelance writers but the drawback is that payment can be small. Don't turn your back on newspapers that don't pay though, particularly if you are just starting out. Publication in local newspapers can provide useful first clippings to keep in your file. Remember, too, that the smaller community newspapers may be run by only one or two people and the editor may be grateful for someone else to call on for the occasional writing task. Many local newspapers come under the umbrella of one of the larger publishing conglomerates, such as Fairfax Media and APN News and Media. Some are members of the New Zealand Community Newspapers Association.

There may be scope for you to approach the editor of your local newspaper with an idea for a regular column on some aspect of local interest (e.g., gardening, local history). The features sections of many larger local newspapers cover a range of topics such as food, sport, motoring, lifestyles, home renovations and building. Local news and items of interest to readers in the newspaper's target area are always welcomed. Often a letter of enquiry to the editor will be useful. If you can come up with an idea around which an editor can build an advertising feature (say, an anniversary for a local industry or community organisation), that may be a good way to get him or her interested. Newspapers servicing rural areas often have opportunities for articles on farming or agricultural features, and these, too, can be turned into good advertising draws for editors.

Community newspapers may provide a good opportunity for the publication of quality black and white or colour photographs, as long as the subject is well known or of local interest.

The golden rule for editors of community newspapers is to keep it local. This should be your maxim too, if you are considering writing for them. If you are interested in entering this market, a useful book to consult is *Writing for Newspapers* by J. Eagles (Auckland, New Zealand Community Newspapers Association, 1985), available from the reference section of your local library. The following list, for space reasons, does not contain guidelines for content. It is a comprehensive listing of contact addresses and numbers only. Prospective contributors should ensure they are familiar with the style and content of their particular target newspaper before submitting material.

> *Useful websites:*
> New Zealand Community Newspapers Association: www.cna.org.nz
> Fairfax Media: www.fairfaxnz.co.nz
> APN News and Media: www.apn.com.au

Akaroa Mail
P.O. Box 84, Kaiapoi.
Tel (03) 327 7622 Fax (03) 327 5500
Email michael@akaroamail.co.nz
Website www.akaroamail.co.nz
Akaroa and Banks Peninsula districts, published fortnightly.

Ashburton's The Courier
P.O. Box 12, Ashburton.
Tel (03) 308 7664 Fax (03) 308 4500
Email ashburton@alliedpress.co.nz
Website www.alliedpress.co.nz
Weekly on Tuesdays, mid-Canterbury.

The Aucklander
P.O. Box 32, Auckland. Tel (09) 373 6969 Fax (09) 373 6583
Website www.theaucklander.co.nz
Weekly, with nine Auckland regional editions – North, Shore, West, East, Central, City, Tamaki, South and Papakura

Auckland City Harbour News
Private Bag 56-910, Dominion Road, Mt Eden, Auckland.
Tel (09) 630 5419 Fax (09) 630 5435
Email edcl@snl.co.nz
Website www.stuff.co.nz/auckland
Inner-city Auckland, published Wednesday and Friday.

Barrier Bulletin
P.O. Box 57, Okiwi, Great Barrier Island.
Tel (09) 429 0084 Fax (09) 429 0126
Email barrierbulletin@iconz.co.nz
News from Great Barrier Island, published twice monthly.

The Bay Chronicle
P.O. Box 392, Kerikeri. Tel (09) 4077218
Email kerikeri.editor@snl.co.nz
Website www.bayofislands.co.nz/chronicle
Bay of Islands and Kerikeri. Weekly.

Bay News
Private Bag 12-002, Tauranga. Tel (07) 578 3059 Fax (07) 577 3158
Email bnews@bopp.co.nz
Tauranga and district, weekly.

Bay Weekend
P.O. Box 243, Whakatane. Tel (07) 308 8129 Fax (07) 307 0719
Email markdawson@whakatane.beacon.co.nz
Weekly 'lifestyle' paper for the eastern Bay of Plenty area.

Bays Times
P.O. Box 259-243, Greenmount, Manukau 2141.
Tel (09) 538 0050 Fax (09) 271 8070
Email editor@times.co.nz
Website www.times.co.nz
Auckland suburbs, published monthly.

Blenheim Sun
P.O. Box 634, Blenheim. Tel (03) 577 7868 Fax (03) 577 7863
Email news@blenheimsun.co.nz
Blenheim area. Weekly

Bush Telegraph
P.O. Box 5470, Pahiatua. Tel (06) 376 8274 Fax (06) 376 6711
Email editorial@bushtele.co.nz
Pahiatua, Dannevirke and Woodville, published weekly on Mondays.

Cambridge Edition
P.O. Box 372, Cambridge. Tel (07) 827 3840 Fax (07) 827 4043
Email cambridge.editor@wrcn.co.nz
Cambridge and Matamata, published weekly on Wednesdays.

Canterbury Times
P.O. Box 1467, Christchurch. Tel (03) 379 7100 Fax (03) 366 0180
Email communities@starcanterbury.co.nz

South-western suburbs of Christchurch and rural central Canterbury, published weekly every Tuesday.

Capital Times
P.O. Box 9202, Wellington. Tel (04) 385 1426 Fax (04) 385 1436
Email editor@captimes.co.nz
Website www.captimes.co.nz
Wellington inner-city suburbs, published weekly on Wednesdays.

Central Canterbury News
P.O. Box 114, Rangiora. Tel 0800 330330 Fax (03) 313 5487
Email sandra.stewartr@press.co.nz
Central Canterbury, published weekly.

Central Districts Farmer
P.O. Box 190, Feilding. Tel (06) 323 5839 Fax (06) 350 9541
Email cdfarmer@msl.co.nz
Rural news for the Manawatu region. Published monthly.

Central Hawke's Bay Mail
P.O. Box 21, Waipukurau. Tel (06) 858 8166 Fax (06) 858 8959
Email editorial@chbmail.co.nz
Website www.apn.co.nz
Central Hawke's Bay, published on Tuesdays.

Central Leader
Private Bag 56-910, Dominion Rd, Mt Eden, Auckland.
Tel (09) 630 5419 Fax (09) 630 5432
Email edcl@snl.co.nz
Website www.stuff.co.nz
Mount Albert, Mount Roskill, Mount Eden, Epsom, Onehunga and Balmoral in Auckland, published twice a week.

Central Otago News
P.O. Box 91, Alexandra. Tel (03) 440 0030 Fax (03) 440 0047
Email lynda.van.kempen@thenews.co.nz
Central Otago, published on Tuesdays and Thursdays.

Christchurch Star
P.O. Box 1467, Christchurch. Tel (03) 379 7100 Fax (03) 366 0180
Email communities@chstar.co.nz
Christchurch and suburbs, published on Wednesdays and Fridays.

Clutha Leader
P.O. Box 45, Balclutha. Tel (03) 418 1115 Fax (03) 418 1173
Email balclutha@stl.co.nz
Balclutha, Milton and Clinton, published weekly

Coastal News
P.O. Box 277, Whangamata. Tel (07) 865 8078 Fax (09) 865 8075
Email coastal.news@bopp.co.nz
Whangamata and coastal areas, published on Thursdays.

The Coaster
P.O. Box 79, Orewa. Tel (09) 426 5024 Fax (09) 426 9078
Email g.dobson@snl.co.nz
Hibiscus Coast and Albany areas, published weekly on Wednesdays.

Coast to Coast Courier
P.O. Box 91, Warkworth. Tel (09) 423 8002
Wellsford and North Auckland, published weekly on Wednesdays.

Cook Strait News
P.O. Box 13-089, Johnsonville, Wellington.
Tel (04) 478 3469 Fax (04) 477 0012
Wellington's eastern and southern suburbs, published weekly on Mondays.

Country
46 Broadway, Matamata. Tel (07) 888 7011 Fax (07) 888 5340
Email matamata.editor@wrcn.co.nz
Published monthly.

The Courier
P.O. Box 179, Timaru. Tel (03) 687 9228 Fax (03) 687 9228
Email timaru@couriernews.co.nz
Website www.alliedpress.co.nz
Timaru region. Weekly. Also *Country Courier* – published monthly for Moeraki/Selwyn River area.

Dargaville and District News
P.O. Box 313, Dargaville. Tel (09) 439 0607 Fax (09) 439 6611
Email dargaville.editor@icn.co.nz
Website www.stuff.co.nz
Published weekly on Wednesdays.

Devonport Flagstaff
P.O. Box 32-275, Devonport, Auckland.
Tel (09) 445 0060 Fax (09) 445 1907
Email rdrent@kiwilink.co.nz
Devonport and surrounding suburbs, published fortnightly on Wednesdays.

Discover Marlborough & Nelson Region
P.O. Box 242, Blenheim. Tel (03) 578 6059
Marlborough & Nelson region, four issues published a year.

Dunedin Star
P.O. Box 517, Dunedin. Tel (03) 479 3505 Fax (03) 474 7426
Website www.alliedpress.co.nz
Dunedin city area, Mosgiel and Port Chalmers, published weekly.

East and Bays Courier
Private Bag 92-185, Penrose, Auckland.
Tel (09) 525 1133 Fax (09) 525 3799
Email edeb@snl.co.nz
Website www.stuff.co.nz
Auckland's eastern suburbs, published biweekly.

East Waikato Country
46 Broadway, Matamata. Tel (07) 888 7011 Fax (07) 888 5340
Published monthly for Matamata-Piako and all eastern Waikato districts.

Eastbourne Herald
P.O. Box 28-127, Wellington 6150.
Tel (04) 475 5039
Email herold@pencom.co.nz
Eastbourne and Eastern Bays, published once a month.

Eastern Bay News
P.O. Box 683, Whakatane. Tel (07) 308 8300 Fax (07) 307 0567
Email shirley.whitwell@easternbaynews.co.nz
Whakatane, Kawerau and Opitiki region, published weekly.

Eastern Courier
Private Bag 38-312, Howick, Auckland.
Tel (09) 535 9660 Fax (09) 535 9664
Email ec@snl.co.nz
Website www.stuff.co.nz
Mount Wellington to Bucklands Beach area, and also rural areas east of Auckland, published twice a week.

Farm Review
P.O. Box 46, Timaru. Tel (03) 684 4129 Fax (03) 688 1042
Email pix@timaruherald.co.nz
Timaru, Ashburton, Palmerston and Mount Cook areas, published on Tuesdays with the Timaru Herald.

Feilding Herald
P.O. Box 190, Feilding. Tel (06) 323 5839 Fax (06) 323 9479
Email feilding.herald@msl.co.nz
Website www.stuff.co.nz
Feilding and its surrounding rural districts, published twice a week on Tuesdays (as the *Feilding Herald* and *Rangitikei Mail*) and Thursdays.

Fiordland Focus
P.O. Box 175, Te Anau. Tel and Fax (03) 249 7177
Email fiordlandfocus@xtra.co.nz
Fiordland district news, published every third Wednesday.

Franklin County News
P.O. Box 14, Pukekohe. Tel (09) 237 0400 Fax (09) 238 9744
Email franklin.editor@wrcn.co.nz
Website www.stuff.co.nz
Franklin County and Raglan, published on Tuesdays and Thursdays.

The Guardian (Motueka-Tasman-Golden Bay)
19 Wallace Street, Motueka. Tel (03) 528 2088 Fax (03) 528 2089
Email guardian.motueka@xtra.co.nz
Published weekly.

The Guardian (Palmerston North)
P.O. Box 1863, Palmerston North. Tel (06) 357 5053 Fax (06) 356 5058
Email editorial@guardiannews.co.nz
Palmerston North, Feilding and Ashhurst, published on Thursdays.

Gulf News
P.O. Box 5, Oneroa, Waiheke Island. Tel (09) 372 5055 Fax (09) 372 5029
Email editor@waihekegulfnews.co.nz
Website www.waihekegulfnews.co.nz
Waiheke Island, published weekly.

Hamilton This Week
P.O. Box 1547, Hamilton. Tel (07) 834 4650 Fax (07) 834 4651
Hamilton and districts, published weekly.

Hamilton Press
Private Bag 3086, Hamilton. Tel (07) 849 6180 Fax (07) 849 9594
Email hamilton.press@wrcn.co.nz
Hamilton city area, published weekly.

Hastings Leader
113 Karamu Road North, Hastings. Tel (06) 878 7670 Fax (06) 878 1117
Email leader@hbtoday.co.nz
Hastings, Havelock North and surrounding districts, published weekly.

Hauraki Herald
P.O. Box 363, Thames. Tel (07) 868 8850 Fax (07) 868 8265
Email hauraki.editor@wrcn.co.nz
Hauraki Plains and Coromandel Peninsula, published Tuesdays and Fridays.

Havelock North Village Press
P.O. Box 8553, Havelock North.
Tel (06) 877 5276 Fax (06) 877 2943
Email vpeditorial@hnvillagepress.co.nz
Southern Hawke's Bay, published fortnightly.

High Country Herald
P.O. Box 46, Timaru. Tel (03) 684 0717 Fax (03) 688 1042
Email hcheditor@timaruherald.co.nz
Website www.stuff.co.nz
Timaru, Ashburton, Palmerston and Mount Cook areas, published on Wednesdays.

Horowhenua Mail
P.O. Box 110, Paraparaumu.
Tel (04) 298 5019 Fax (04) 298 2073
Email editor@kapiti-observer.co.nz
Horowhenua and Kapiti region, published on Thursdays.

Howick and Pakuranga Times
P.O. Box 259-243, Greenmount, Auckland 1730.
Tel (09) 271 8000 Fax (09) 271 8073
Website www.times.co.nz
Howick and Pakuranga, published Mondays and Thursdays.
Also *Howick and Botany Times*, published weekly.

Hurunui News
P.O. Box 86, Amberley.
Tel (03) 314 8335 Fax (03) 314 8071
Email hurunui-news@xtra.co.nz
Rural Canterbury, published fortnightly.

Hutt News
P.O. Box 30-029, Lower Hutt. Tel (04) 570 2040 Fax (04) 566 5485
Email editor@huttnews.co.nz
Lower Hutt, Wainuiomata, Petone and Eastbourne, published on Tuesdays.

Kaikoura Star
P.O. Box 88, Kaikoura. Tel (03) 319 5021 Fax (03) 319 6483
Website www.marlboroughexpress.co.nz
Kaikoura town and district, published weekly on Wednesdays.

Kapi-Mana News
P.O. Box 50-012, Porirua. Tel (04) 237 8118 Fax (04) 237 8552
Email editor@kmananews.co.nz
Porirua, Pukerua Bay, Plimmerton and Tawa areas north of Wellington, published on Tuesdays.

Kapiti Observer
P.O. Box 110, Paraparaumu. Tel (04) 298 5019 Fax (04) 298 2073
Email editor@kapiti-observer.co.nz
Kapiti Coast, published on Mondays and Thursdays.

Katikati Advertiser
14 Main Road, Katikati. Tel (07) 549 0270 Fax (07) 549 0851
Email kknews@bopp.co.nz
Bay of Plenty, published on Tuesdays.

The Leader
P.O. Box 244, Nelson. Tel (03) 546 9005 Fax (03) 546 2705
Email theleader@nelsonmail.co.nz
One edition for Nelson City and another for Richmond–Waimea area, both published weekly on a Thursday.

Local Matters
P.O. Box 701, Warkworth. Tel (09) 425 9068 Fax (09) 425 9088
Email localmatters@extra.co.nz
Rodney district, published monthly.

Look North
P.O. Box 1, Kaikohe. Tel (09) 401 0123 Fax (09) 401 2129
Email northern.editor@wrcn.co.nz
Published in October, December, February and April.

Manukau Courier
P.O. Box 76-400, Manukau City. Tel (09) 262 4700 Fax (09) 262 4728
Email edmc@snl.co.nz
Manukau and South Auckland areas, published three times a week.

Manukau Times
P.O. Box 259 243, Greenmount, Manukau.
Tel (09) 271 8000 Fax (09) 271 8073
Manukau region, published weekly.

Matamata Chronicle
46 Broadway, Matamata. Tel (07) 888 7011 Fax (07) 888 5340
Email matamata.editor@wrcn.co.nz
Matamata and Piako regions, published on Tuesdays.

Midweek
P.O. Box 259-243, Greenmount, Manukau.
Tel (09) 271 8000 Fax (09) 271 8073
Email emmas@midweekl.co.nz
Website www.times.co.nz
South Auckland suburbs, published weekly.

Motueka–Golden Bay News
P.O. Box 244, Nelson. Tel (03) 548 7079 Fax (03) 528 6129
Motueka region, published on Thursdays.

Mount and Papamoa Times
P.O. Box 5164, Mount Maunganui. Tel (07) 575 8666 Fax (07) 575 8988
Email mount.editor@icn.co.nz
Mt Maunganui and Papamoa area, published weekly on Thursdays.

Mountain Scene
P.O. Box 299, Queenstown. Tel (03) 442 7000 Fax (03) 442 7006
Email ferrisg@scene.co.nz
Website www.scene.co.nz
Queenstown and surrounding areas, featuring regular news.
Published weekly.

Napier Courier
39 Tennyson Street, Napier. Tel (06) 834 3235 Fax (06) 835 9573
Napier and Taradale, published weekly.

Napier Mail
P.O. Box 222, Napier. Tel (06) 835 5553 Fax (06) 833 7443
Email editorial@napiermail.co.nz
Website www.napiermail.co.nz
Napier region, published weekly.

Newslink
P.O. Box 805, Invercargill. Tel (03) 211 1051 Fax (03) 214 3713
Email communities@stl.co.nz
Gore and eastern areas of Southland, published weekly.

North Canterbury News
P.O. Box 1467, Christchurch. Tel (03) 379 7100 Fax (03) 366 0180
Email communities@chstar.co.nz
Rangiora, Kaiapoi, Cheviot and surrounding districts, published weekly on Tuesday.

North Harbour News
P.O. Box 33-235, Takapuna, Auckland.
Tel (09) 489 4189 Fax (09) 486 6700
Email nsnews@snl.co.nz
Auckland's northern city suburbs, published weekly.

North Shore Times
P.O. Box 33-235, Takapuna, Auckland. Tel (09) 489 4189 Fax (09) 486 6700
Email nsnews@snl.co.nz
North Shore area of Auckland, published three times a week.

North Taranaki Midweek
P.O. Box 777, New Plymouth. Tel (06) 759 0800 Fax (06) 759 0814
Website www.fairfax.co.nz
New Plymouth and North Taranaki, published on Wednesdays.

North Waikato News
P.O. Box 234, Huntly. (07) 828 7484 Fax (07) 828 8877
Email huntly.editor@wrcn.co.nz
Published weekly on Wednesdays.

Northern Courier
P.O. Box 50-102, Porirua, Wellington.
Tel (04) 237 3220 Fax (04) 237 9249
Email editor@prestigemedia.co.nz
Website www.prestigemedia.co.nz
Northern suburbs of Wellington from Pukerua Bay to Ngaio, published fortnightly on Tuesdays.

Northern News
P.O. Box 1, Kaikohe. Tel (09) 405 2040 Fax (09) 401 2129
Email northern.editor@icn.co.nz
Northland and the Bay of Islands, published weekly.

Northern Outlook
P.O. Box 114, Rangiora. Tel (03) 313 6183 Fax (03) 313 5487
Email outlooknews@xtra.co.nz
North Canterbury towns and rural districts, published twice a week.

Northland Age
P.O. Box 45, Kaitaia. Tel (09) 408 0330 Fax (09) 408 2955
Email nor-age@xtra.co.nz
Website www.northnz.co.nz
Mangonui and Hokianga regions, published twice a week on Tuesdays and Thursdays.

Nor'West News
P.O. Box 46, Kumeu. Tel (09) 412 8589 Fax (09) 412 7806
Email nwn@snl.co.nz
North Auckland and region, published weekly.

Opotiki News
P.O. Box 51, Opotiki. Tel (07) 315 6106 Fax (07) 315 6494
Email news@whakatanebeacon.co.nz
Opotiki and surrounding districts, published Tuesdays and Thursdays.

Opunake & Coastal News
P.O. Box 74, Opunake. Tel and fax (06) 761 7016

Email opunakecoastalnews@paradise.net.nz
Published fortnightly on Thursday.

Otago–Southland Farmer
P.O. Box 105, Mosgiel. Tel (03) 489 7123 Fax (03) 489 7668
Email Suzanne.muir@stl.co.nz
Rural news for Otago and Southland farmers, published fortnightly.

Papakura Courier
P.O. Box 76-400, Manukau City. Tel (09) 262 4700 Fax (09) 262 4728
Email edmc@snl.co.nz
Takanini, Papakura, Bombay and Ramarama in south Auckland, published weekly.

Petone Herald
P.O. Box 50-102, Wellington.
Tel (04) 237 3220 Fax (04) 237 9249
Email editor@prestigemedia.co.nz
Website www.prestigemedia.co.nz
Petone area, published fortnightly on Tuesdays.

Piako Post
P.O. Box 125, Morrinsville. Tel (07) 889 7099 Fax (07) 889 6572
Email piako.editor@wrcn.co.nz
Morrinsville, Te Aroha, Piako and outlying areas, published weekly on Wednesdays.

Pohutukawa Coast Times
P.O. Box 5, Beachlands, Auckland.
Tel (09) 536 5715 Fax (09) 536 5714
Email pctimes@maxnet.co.nz
Maraetai and Beachlands area, published weekly on Fridays.

The Queenstown Mirror
P.O. Box 770, Queenstown. Tel (03) 441 0690 Fax (03) 442 7886
Two editions, one for Central Otago and one for Queenstown Lakes District, both published on Wednesdays.

Rangitikei Mail
P.O. Box 190, Feilding. Tel (06) 323 5839 Fax (06) 350 9541
Email liz.brook@msl.co.nz
Rangitikei district, Marton, Bulls and Ohakea, published weekly.

River City Press
P.O. Box 325, Wanganui. Tel (06) 345 3666 Fax (06) 345 2644
Email rivercitypress@xtra.co.nz
Wanganui city, published on Thursdays.

Rodney Times
P.O. Box 636, Warkworth. Tel (09) 426 8169 Fax (09) 425 7765
Email g.dobson@snl.co.nz
Hibiscus Coast, Albany, Kumeu and Whangaparaoa areas, published twice a week on Tuesdays and Thursdays.

Rotorua Review
P.O. Box 2244, Rotorua. Tel (07) 348 0045 Fax (07) 346 2877
Email rotorua.editor@wrcn.co.nz
Rotorua city and area, published weekly on Tuesdays.

Ruapehu Bulletin
P.O. Box 122, Ohakune. Tel (06) 385 8532 Fax (06) 385 8622
Email ed@ruapehubulletin.co.nz
Waiouru and Ohakune districts, published on Tuesdays.

Ruapehu Press
P.O. Box 190, Taumaraunui. Tel (07) 895 5841 Fax (07) 895 8765
Email ed@ruapehubulletin.co.nz
Central Plateau region, published weekly.

Saturday Express
P.O. Box 242, Blenheim. Tel (03) 577 2950 Fax (03) 577 2953
Email editorial@marlexpress.co.nz
Published weekly on Saturdays.

South Taranaki Star
P.O. Box 428 Hawera. Tel (06) 278 5139 Fax (06) 278 5458
Email hwastar.edit@tnl.co.nz
www.stuff.co.nz
South Taranaki and Stratford, published weekly.

South Waikato News
P.O. Box 89, Tokoroa. Tel (07) 886 9159 Fax (07) 886 5347
Email swaikato.editor@wrcn.co.nz
Website www.stuff.co.nz
Tokoroa, Putaruru and surrounding districts, published weekly on Wednesdays.

Southern Rural Life
P.O. Box 517, Dunedin. Tel (03) 477 4760 x 8585 Fax (03) 474 7426
Website www.alliedpress.co.nz
Otago/Southland, published weekly.

Southland Express
P.O. Box 354, Invercargill. Tel (03) 218 4818 Fax (03) 214 4179
Email editorial.@southlandexpress.co.nz

Website www.southlandexpress.co.nz
North from Invercargill and Bluff to Te Anau and Riversdale, published weekly.

Star Community
P.O. Box 1467, Christchurch. Tel (03) 377 2450 Fax (03) 364 7480
Southern suburbs of Christchurch, including the Port Hills and Lyttelton, published every Monday.

Stratford Press
P.O. Box 300, Stratford. Tel (06) 765 5471 Fax (06) 765 5978
Email editor@stratfordpress.co.nz
Website www.stratfordpress.co.nz
Central Taranaki area, published on Wednesdays.

Taihape Times
P.O. Box 30, Taihape. Tel (06) 388 0639 Fax (06) 388 0659
Email taihape.times@xtra.co.nz
Raetihi to Hunterville, published weekly on Tuesdays.

Taieri Herald
P.O. Box 105, Mosgiel. Tel (03) 211 1051 Fax (03) 314 3713
Email communities@stl.co.nz
Website www.taieri.herald@stl.co.nz
Mosgiel, Fairfield and Green Island, published weekly on Tuesdays.

Tamaki and Districts Times
P.O. Box 259-243, Greenmount, Manukau.
Tel (09) 271 8000 Fax (09) 271 8073
The south Auckland area around Tamaki, published weekly.

Taupo Times
P.O. Box 205, Taupo. Tel (07) 378 9060 Fax (07) 378 0247
Email times.news@wrcn.co.nz
Website www.stuff.co.nz
Taupo and Turangi areas, published three times a week on Tuesdays, Thursdays and Fridays.

Taupo Weekender
P.O. Box 108, Taupo. Tel (07) 376 1360 Fax (07) 378 0020
Email info@taupoweekender.co.nz
Taupo and Turangi areas, published a week on Thursdays.

Te Awamutu Courier
P.O. Box 1, Te Awamutu. Tel (07) 871 5151 Fax (07) 871 3675
Te Awamutu, Waipa and Otorohanga, published a week on Tuesdays and Thursdays.

Timaru's The Courier
P.O. Box 179, Timaru. Tel (03) 687 9228 Fax (03) 687 9228
Email timaru@couriernews.co.nz
Website www.alliedpress.co.nz
Timaru and district, published on Thursdays.

The Tribune
P.O. Box 3, Palmerston North. Tel (06) 356 9839 Fax (06) 350 9836
Email tribune@msl.co.nz
Palmerston North City, published weekly on Sundays.

Turangi Chronicle
P.O. Box 265, Turangi. Tel (07) 386 8335 Fax (07) 386 5421
Email taupo_weekender@wilsonandhorton.co.nz
Turangi area, published weekly.

Upper Hutt Leader
P.O. Box 40-001, Upper Hutt. Tel (04) 528 9654 Fax (04) 528 3021
Email editor@uhleader.co.nz
Upper Hutt and Hutt Valley, published on Wednesdays.

The Waiheke Week
P.O. Box 378, Oneroa, Waiheke. Tel (09) 372 2201 Fax (09) 372 2197
Email info@waihekeweek.co.nz
Website www.waihekeweek.co.nz
Waiheke Island news published weekly on Thursday.

Waihi Leader
47 Seddon St, Waihi. Tel (07) 863 8887 Fax (07) 863 8945
Email reporters.waihileader@xtra.co.nz
Waihi and outlying areas, published on Tuesdays.

Waikato This Week
P.O. Box 1547, Hamilton. Tel (07) 838 3386 Fax (07) 834 4651
Hamilton, Cambridge and Raglan, published weekly on Thursdays.

Waimate Advertiser
P.O. Box 15, Waimate. Tel & Fax (03) 689 7345
Waimate borough, published on Wednesdays and Fridays.

Wairarapa Midweek
P.O. Box 445, Masterton. Tel (06) 378 9999 Fax (06) 378 0966
Website www.times.age.co.nz
Masterton and Wairarapa, published weekly on Tuesdays.

Wairarapa News
P.O. Box 902, Masterton. Tel (06) 370 5690 Fax (06) 370 5699

Email editor@wainews.co.nz
Website www.stuff.co.nz
Wairarapa, published weekly on Wednesday.

Wairoa Star
P.O. Box 41, Wairoa. Tel (06) 838 7194 Fax (06) 838 6973
Email editorial@wairoastar.co.nz
Website www.wairoastar.co.nz
Wairoa and districts, published on Tuesdays and Thursdays.

Waitomo News
P.O. Box 279, Te Kuiti. Tel (07) 878 1188 Fax (07) 878 1187
Website www.waitomonews.co.nz
Otorohanga and Waitomo, published Tuesdays and Thursdays.

Waiuku and Districts Post
P.O. Box 374, Waiuku. Tel (09) 235 7835 Fax (09) 235 7834
Email waiuku.editorial@xtra.co.nz
Waiuku area, published weekly on Tuesdays.

Wanaka Sun
P.O. Box 697, Wanaka. Tel (03) 443 5252 Fax (03) 443 5250
Website www.wanaka.co.nz
Wanaka district, published weekly on Tuesday.

Wanganui Midweek
P.O. Box 433, Wanganui. Tel (06) 349 0710 Fax (06) 349 0723
Email midweek@wanganuichronicle.co.nz
Bulls, Marton, Hunterville and Wanganui, published weekly.

The Weekender
P.O. Box 1442, Rotorua. Tel (07) 348 6199 Fax (07) 348 0220
Email news@dailypost.co.nz
Rotorua area, published weekly on a Friday.

The Weekly News
P.O. Box 547, Levin. Tel (06) 368 5109 Fax (06) 368 2366
Levin, Otaki and outlying areas, published weekly on Wednesdays.

The Wellingtonian
P.O. Box 3740, Wellington.
Tel (04) 474 0362 Fax (04) 474 0140
Email editor@thewellingtonian.co.nz
Wellington City, published weekly on Thursdays.

The West Coast Messenger
3 Werita St, Greymouth. Tel (03) 768 9456 Fax (03) 768 9455

Email messenger@greystar.co.nz
West Coast and Greymouth, published weekly on Wednesday.

Western Leader
P.O. Box 21-167, Henderson, Auckland.
Tel (09) 837 0340 Fax (09) 837 1760
Email edwl@snl.co.nz
Auckland's western districts, published three times a week.

Whakatane Beacon
P.O. Box 243, Whakatane. Tel (07) 308 8129 Fax (07) 307 0719
Whakatane, Opotiki and Kawerau district, published Tuesdays, Wednesdays and Fridays.

Whangarei Leader
P.O. Box 433, Whangarei. Tel (09) 438 8636 Fax (09) 438 9770
Email whangarei.editor@icn.co.nz
Whangarei City and surrounding suburbs, published weekly on Tuesdays.

Whangarei Report
P.O. Box 1603, Whangarei. Tel & Fax (09) 470 2840
Email editor@thereport.co.nz
Whangarei City and districts, published weekly on Thursdays.

15 Magazines and Periodicals

There are hundreds of magazine titles published in New Zealand at present. The following list has been selected from those magazines on two criteria — circulation size and specialisation. Magazines that have a circulation under about 5,000 copies per issue are not included, as their potential for freelance contributors is small; similarly excluded are magazines that deal with highly technical or specialised areas requiring expert knowledge. Some exceptions have been made to both rules, due to the interesting nature of those particular publications.

In all cases, you should endeavour to get hold of at least two or three recent issues of a magazine before you write for it. This will give you a feel for the style and format of the publication, and will also give you some idea as to whether your writing will be suitable for it. Take note of the subjects dealt with, the approach taken by other writers, their styles, and the general length of articles. It is the editor's job to understand the magazine's target market and to make sure the magazine is filled with what readers want; therefore freelance articles are more likely to be accepted if they meet the editor's requirements. It's worth enquiring beforehand as to whether articles will be accepted by email, or whether the editor prefers 'hard copy' submissions by post accompanied by copy on a disk.

Although the well-known consumer magazines are obvious targets for freelance writers, those beginning a career in writing should aim for the magazines with smaller circulations. Although the fees may be less, the chances of being accepted are higher, and they provide an excellent training ground for writers to amass writing skills, self-confidence and credibility. Neither should you ignore the wide potential that exists in trade publications. These are magazines and periodicals written about an industry by members of that industry — and although they often work on low budgets, a knowledgeable freelancer may well be able to create a niche in the market if he or she is willing to approach editors with ideas and examples of previous work. Styles for trade magazines are invariably matter-of-fact and straightforward; again, you should carefully study potential markets in your particular area of interest. Often, the editor of a trade journal will welcome new ideas and perspectives as long as they are of general appeal to his or her readership.

Finally, it's worth saying that no matter how remote or exclusive a magazine may appear to be, no editor will turn down a great idea — it's up to you to sell it to them.

Useful websites:
Magazine Publishers Association: www.mpa.org.nz
Fairfax Media: www.fairfaxnz.co.nz
ACPMedia: www.acpmedia.co.nz
AGM Publishing Ltd: www.agm.co.nz

AA Directions
P.O. Box 5, Auckland. Tel (09) 377 4660 Fax (09) 357 9975
Email editor@nzaa.co.nz
Website www.aa.co.nz
The official magazine of the New Zealand Automobile Association, *AA Directions* has travel and lifestyle features and articles with news and issues of interest to motorists. Most articles commissioned or written by staff writers.

AdMedia & Fastline
Private Bag 5544, Wellesley Street, Auckland.
Tel (09) 630 1624 Fax (09) 630 1046
Email david@admedia.co.nz. Website www.admedia.co.nz
Admedia is a monthly A4 glossy and *Fastline* is a weekly newsletter posted to all *AdMedia* subscribers. Editor of both is David Gapes — email address as above. A trade journal for those involved in advertising and marketing. Sometimes accepts articles from freelance contributors on relevant news and information for the marketing fraternity, but these need prior discussion with editor. Prefer all submissions, copy, art and photographs by email.

New Zealand Adventure Magazine
PO Box 562, Whangaparaoa. Tel (09) 428 2441 Fax (09) 428 2443
Email p.media@xtra.co.nz
Website www.pacificmedia.co.nz
Adventure activities in New Zealand and around the world.

Air New Zealand Magazine
Private Bag 92-512, Auckland.
Tel (09) 308 2700 Fax (09) 379 2300
Free inflight monthly magazine showcasing the best of NZ business, sport, arts, travel, food, wine and lifestyle. Stable of contributors, with most of the stories commissioned.

Animals' Voice
P.O. Box 432-21. Tel 09 256 7300 Fax (09) 256 7314
Website: www.spca.org.nz
News and information about the SPCA's activities plus stories about animals and care tips. Quarterly.

Architecture NZ
Private Bag 99-915, Newmarket, Auckland.
Tel (09) 846 4068 Fax (09) 846 8742
Email john.walsh@agm.co.nz
News, features and information on the architectural profession and infrastructure related to service sectors involved in building and design. Published bimonthly.

The Juice Arthritis Newsletter
P.O. Box 10-020, Wellington. Tel (04) 472 1427
Website www.arthritis.org.nz
The newsletter of the Arthritis Foundation, featuring news and information on the Foundation's activities, along with material of general interest to arthritis sufferers. Published quarterly. Freelance material welcomed.

Art New Zealand
P.O. Box 10-249, Dominion Road, Auckland 3. Tel & Fax (09) 630 1328
Email editor@art_newzealand.com
A quarterly magazine reviewing the arts scene in New Zealand. Made up of profiles, criticism and news of forthcoming events.

Art News New Zealand
P.O. Box 137-300, Newmarket, Auckland.
Tel (09) 357 6006 Fax (09) 358 0606
Email virginia@artnews.co.nz
Website www.artnews.co.nz
Quarterly arts publication, with profiles, reviews and features.

Asthma Update
P.O. Box 67-066, Mt Eden, Auckland. Tel (09) 630 2293 Fax (09) 623 0774
Email aas@asthma-nz.org.nz
Asthma New Zealand's quarterly magazine, available by subscription, with news and information for people with asthma and allergies.

Australia and New Zealand Apparel
P.O. Box 37-140, Parnell, Auckland. Tel (09) 353 2415 Fax (09) 366 0283
Email paola@4rpl.com
Comprehensive trade magazine covering every aspect of the fashion industry on both sides of the Tasman, including marketing, import, footwear and textiles, wholesale and retail apparel, logistics, technology and recruitment. Published 11 times a year.

Australian Woman's Weekly (NZ edition)
Private Bag 92-512, Wellesley Street, Auckland 1141.
Tel (09) 308 7416 Fax (09) 379 2300
Email aww@acpmagazines.co.nz
News stories, celebrity interviews, beauty and fashion, special features, recipes, crafts and issues relevant to the home front with some New Zealand content. Published monthly.

Beaded Wheels
P.O. Box 13-140, Christchurch. Tel (03) 332 3531
Website www.vcc.org.nz
Specialist motoring enthusiast's magazine, published bimonthly — should be studied closely for style and content before material is submitted. Historical motoring and local historic vehicle interest articles, colour or black and white photographs if space available. Payment is at the editor's discretion; contributions are generally only accepted on a voluntary basis.

Boating New Zealand
P.O. Box 12-965, Penrose, Auckland.
Tel (09) 634 1800 Fax (09) 634 2948
Email rebecca.hayter@boatingnz.co.nz
A full-colour large-format magazine for boating enthusiasts, published monthly. The editor accepts freelance submissions, preferably by hard copy, accompanied by colour photographs or illustrations if appropriate, which may be sent after the article has been accepted. Rates of pay discussed on merit. The editor will accept cruising stories, offshore adventures, technical and other articles that fit the general theme of the publication.

Building Today
P.O. Box 35-343, Browns Bay, Auckland.
Tel (09) 478 4888 Fax (09) 478 4588
Email andrew@buildingtoday.co.nz
The official journal of the New Zealand Registered Master Builders' Federation, this magazine is published monthly, except January. The main focus of the magazine is construction industry news, and includes regular product and project features, along with legal, architecture, science and technology, and business financing columns. Freelance submissions are accepted by way of a preliminary letter to the editor, with project stories and news from around New Zealand preferred. Colour photographs are welcome. Rates of pay for submissions: 25 cents a word.

BWS
P.O. Box 37-140, Parnell, Auckland.
Tel (09) 353 2438 Fax (09) 366 0283
Email edward@4rpl.com
Monthly magazine for liquor resellers. Stories on businesses and people involved with beer, wines and spirits.

Canterbury Today
P.O. Box 1879, Christchurch. Tel (03) 961 5050
Email editor@academy.net.nz
Events, places and people in the Canterbury region. Aimed mainly at visitors to the area.

Canterbury Tourist Times
P.O. Box 90, Belfast 8030, Christchurch.
Tel (03) 323 7019 Fax (03) 323 7029
Email touristtimes@xtra.co.nz
News, information, events, personalities; aimed at tourists.
Seldom uses freelancers.

Classic Driver
P.O. Box 8673, Symonds Street, Auckland.
Tel (09) 369 5412 Fax (09) 369 5422
Email editor@classicdriver.co.nz
Website www.drivermagazine.co.nz
Bi-monthly devoted to classic cars and historic motorsport.

Cleo
Private Bag 92-512, Wellesley Street, Auckland.
Tel (09) 308 2735 Fax (09) 302 0667
Email cleo@acpmedia.co.nz
Women's lifestyle. Content mainly from overseas or supplied by staff writers.

Commercial Horticulture
P.O. Box 26-269, Epsom, Auckland.
Tel (09) 358 2749 Fax (09) 358 2741
Email comhort@nursery.net.nz
Website www.nursery.net.nz
News and developments for those involved in commercial horticulture throughout New Zealand.

Computerworld New Zealand
P.O. Box 6813, Auckland.
Tel (09) 377 9902 Fax (09) 377 4604
Email paul_brislen@computerworld.co.nz
News weekly about computers, software, hardware, industry news, new developments and features of interest to computer users.

Country-Wide
P.O. Box 529, Feilding.
Tel (06) 323 7104 Fax (06) 323 7101
Email info@country-wide.co.nz
Website www.country-wide.co.nz

Farm management topics: research, development, animal health, pasture management and livestock. Farming and agriculture.

Crème
P.O. Box 90-119, Auckland Mail Centre.
Tel (09) 373 9400 Fax (09) 373 9401
Email editor@crememagazine.co.nz
Website www.crememagazine.co.nz
Creme magazine is a New Zealand teenage magazine focused on music, films, television, local and international celebrities and broader teen issues including health and fitness, beauty, travel and relationships. Other features include website, album and movie reviews, role models, quizzes and horoscopes. The editor does accept material and ideas from freelance writers, but most contributors are tertiary students studying in journalism who wish to get their work published for free.

Cuisine
P.O. Box 6341, Auckland 1036.
Tel (09) 353 1010 Fax (09) 353 1020
Email admin@cuisine.co.nz
Website www.cuisine.co.nz
Cuisine focuses on food, wine, travel and associated good living in a glossy, high production value format. The bimonthly magazine rarely uses unsolicited manuscripts, but usually commissions writers to work on specific topics. A preliminary letter to the editor is therefore essential — if the idea is one that will work, then illustrations, payment and deadlines can be discussed.

Curl
PO Box 562, Whangaparaoa. Tel (09) 428 2441 Fax (09) 428 2443
Email lynne@curl.co.nz
Website www.curl.co.nz
Female ocean lifestyle title. Best surfing women in NZ and internationally, fashion, skin care, etc.

The Cut
Private Bag 37-745, Parnell, Auckland.
Tel (09) 377 2114 Fax (09) 377 2115
Email thecut@armadapublishing
Monthly publication focusing on golf. Reviews of equipment and courses.

Dairyman
P.O. Box 4233, AMC, Auckland.
Tel (09) 523 5056 Fax (09) 524 1170
Email dairyman@ruralpress.com
News and general interest articles for dairy farmers and those involved in the trade. Published monthly.

Deals On Wheels
P.O. Box 9251, Wellesley Street, Auckland 1141.
Tel (09) 308 2833 Fax (09) 302 7661
Website www.dealsonwheels.co.nz
Monthly automobile publication. Specialising in trucks and heavy equipment.

The Deer Farmer
P.O. Box 11-092, Wellington. Tel (021) 388 031 Fax (04) 970 4586
Email deereditor@wham.co.nz
Website www.deerfarmer.co.nz
News, market information, technology and specialist articles for deer farmers. Published monthly.

DEMM
P.O. Box 65-092, Mairangi Bay, Auckland.
Tel (09) 478 4771 Fax (09) 478 4779
Email cathy@adrenalin.co.nz
Website www.demm.co.nz
Monthly publication focusing on engineering and manufacturing.

Destinations
74 Jervois Road, Herne Bay, Auckland.
Tel (09) 360 4096 Fax (09) 360 4097
Email bruce@destinationsmagazine.com
Website www.destinationsmagazine.com
Glossy quarterly publication focusing on travel and leisure.
Also Wine, Golf, Island and Ocean Destinations editions published annually. Top quality colour digital images or transparencies a must for submissions. Targeted at affluent readers who are seasoned travellers rather than tourists. Stories should have a distinctive style and angle and be no more than 1500 words.

Dish
P.O. Box 91-344, Auckland Mail Centre.
Tel (09) 360 6424 Fax (09) 358 7291
Email dish@jonespublishing.co.nz
Website www.dish.co.nz
Quarterly magazine for foodies, featuring recipes and the latest in cookware and kitchen tools. Most of the content is commissioned.

Dive New Zealand & Dive Pacific
P.O. Box 42-020, Orakei, Auckland. Tel (09) 521 0680 Fax (09) 521 3675
Email divenz@divenewzealand.co.nz
Website www.divenewzealand.com
Dive New Zealand magazine is targeted to the New Zealand market while *Dive Pacific* is targeted to Australia and the South Pacific region.

In New Zealand it is the only magazine dedicated to the sport of scuba diving and related activities. The magazine features articles on such subjects as: dive locations around New Zealand, Australia and the Pacific; marine subjects such as marine life, conservation and research; local and international news; boat tests; spearfishing; shipwrecks; underwater photography; dive medicine. Writers are invited to visit the website for detailed information for articles, submissions and payment. Articles are to be supplied preferably via email or hard copy with a complementary disk, pictures via email or originals/duplicates posted to the office.

Driver
P.O. Box 8673, Symonds Street, Auckland.
Tel (09) 369 5412
Email editor@drivermagazine.co.nz
Monthly motor magazine.

Education Weekly
P.O. Box 26-302, Epsom, Auckland. Tel (09) 849 7100 Fax (09) 849 7103
Email eduvac@millspublish.co.nz
In-depth news for teachers, featuring material on curriculum developments and other educational news. Publishes recruitment positions for schools and ECC. Weekly.

Electrical and Automation Technology
P.O. Box 65-092, Mairangi Bay, Auckland.
Tel (09) 478 4771 Fax (09) 478 4779
Email cathy@adrenalin.co.nz
Website www.electricalautomation.co.nz
Covers topics related to the New Zealand electrical and industrial automation industries, including independent reviews of industry activities

ElectroLink
P.O. Box 91-300, Auckland Mail Centre, Auckland.
Tel (09) 302 8360 Fax (09) 302 8362
Email neil@electrolink.co.nz
Website www.electrolink.co.nz
Business and management news and information relating to New Zealand's electro-technology industries. Lighting, industrial automation, datacomms, refrigeration/air conditioning, electrical engineering. Published bimonthly.

Essentially Food
P.O. Box 37-140, Auckland. Tel (09) 358 4465 Fax (09) 366 0283
Email tamara@4rpl.com
Website www.4rpl.com
Bimonthly magazine for New World customers. Recipes and stories on food, beverages and people working in this area.

Eye Magazine
P.O. Box 90-693 AMC, Auckland 1142.
Tel (09) 306 0921 Fax (09) 306 0922
Email Vanessa@eyemagazine.co.nz
Website www.eyemagazine.co.nz
Quarterly lifestyle magazine for fashionable living.

Fashion Quarterly
Private Bag 92-512, Wellesley Street, Auckland 1141.
Tel (09) 308 2940 Fax (09) 379 2300
Email fq@acpmagazines.co.nz
A glossy quarterly featuring international trends and local designers, profiles and features. First-class fashion photography. Mostly written by staff writers or commissioned.

Fish and Game New Zealand
P.O. Box 12-965, Penrose, Auckland. Tel (09) 634 1800 Fax (09) 634 2948
Email office@fishnz.co.nz
Website www.fishandgame.org.nz
Eighty per cent of the magazine is devoted to fly fishing and the remaining 20 per cent to game bird hunting. Published quarterly.

FMCG
P.O. Box 37-140, Parnell, Auckland. Tel (09) 353 2430 Fax (09) 366 0283
Email john@4rpl.co.nz
Monthly trade magazine which covers everything in the NZ food and beverage industry right through to the supermarket shelf and taking into account packaging, design and logistics along the way. There are stories on products, companies and people.

Food and Beverage
P.O. Box 9596, Newmarket, Auckland. Tel (09) 529 3000 Fax (09) 529 3001
Email donk@pplmedia.co.nz
A monthly trade magazine for the food, catering and supply business. Most articles are commissioned but the editor will consider submissions.

FoodService Magazine
P.O. Box 37-140, Parnell, Auckland.
Tel (09) 358 4465 Fax (09) 366 0283
The widest-reaching monthly trade publication within the food service and wider hospitality industry, covering issues, products and trends. Monthly publication distributed around the country to restaurants, bars, clubs, RSAs and other food service outlets with varied articles designed to cover the changing and growing nature of the business.

New Zealand Food Technology
P.O. Box 33-146, Takapuna, Auckland.

Tel (09) 486 0077 Fax (09) 486 0078
Email sbest@hayleymedia.com
Website www.foodtechnology.co.nz
News and information for researchers and industry people concerning developments and innovations in food technology.

Foodtown Magazine
P.O. Box 90-945, AMSC, Auckland. Tel (09) 368 1258 Fax (09) 368 1257
Bimonthly magazine for Foodtown and Woolworths customers featuring recipes, new products, wine reviews, and lifestyle features such as travel and beauty.

Forest & Bird
P.O. Box 631, Wellington. Tel (04) 385 7374 Fax (04) 385 7373
Email m.szabo@forestandbird.org.nz
Website www.forestandbird.org.nz
Forest & Bird is the quarterly magazine of the Royal Forest and Bird Protection Society of New Zealand Inc, circulated directly to members. It is a 48-page, heavily illustrated, full-colour A4 magazine, dedicated to natural history, conservation, and the outdoors. Most articles are contributed by members and experts but occasional freelance articles are used. Contact the editor first as the magazine has very specific editorial requirements.

Girlfriend
P.O. Box 1467, Auckland. Tel (09) 979 2700 Fax (09) 979 2776
Email vicki.lee@pacificmagazines.co.nz
Girlfriend magazine is primarily targeted at the 13-19 age group and covers all the latest celebrity gossip, plus real-life issues, features, fashion and beauty as well as offering teenage advice. *Girlfriend* magazine is published on a monthly basis. The editor is open to submissions of relevant NZ-based celebrity and real-life stories.

Good Teacher Magazine
P.O. Box 5531, Mt Maunganui 3150.
Tel 021 798 868 Fax (07) 542 5258
Email barisa-holdings@xtra.co.nz
Publication for educators. Distributed quarterly to all New Zealand schools, some early childhood centres and most tertiary institutions.

Grapevine
Private Bag 92-124, Auckland. Tel (09) 813 4956 Fax (09) 813 4957
Email info@grapevine.org.nz
Website www. grapevine.org.nz
Grapevine is delivered free to selected homes all over New Zealand. The magazine uses freelance writers often, usually commissioned or regularly retained, but may sometimes use unsolicited contributions. Writers should submit material to the editor.

Grill
P.O. Box 5544, Wellesley Street, Auckland.
Tel (09) 630 1624 Fax (09) 630 2307
Email editor@grill.co.nz
Bimonthly magazine for NZ's hospitality professionals.
Equipment, food, wine.

Grower
P.O. Box 10-232, Wellington.
Tel (04) 472 3795 Fax (04) 471 2861
Email paterson@thegrower.co.nz
Website www.thegrower.co.nz
Horticultural news for the vegetable industry and exporters.

Gunshot
P.O. Box 5355, Christchurch. Tel (03) 352 8577 Fax (03) 352 0077
Email nzcta@xtra.co.nz Website www.nzclaytarget.org.nz
Hunters and gun enthusiasts; news and information on equipment and innovations.

Her Business magazine
P. O. Box 65, Morrinsville. Tel (07) 889 4053 Fax (07) 889 4058
Email herbusiness@xtra.co.nz
Website www.herbusinessmagazine.com
Her Business magazine is a bimonthly, nation-wide magazine for women in business featuring a range of articles on business management advice, self-development, topics of interest, well-being and businesswomen's profiles. Well-written and relevant freelance submissions are welcomed. Send a preliminary email to the editor before submitting an article.

Heritage New Zealand
P.O. Box 2629, Wellington. Tel (04) 472 4341 Fax (04) 499 0669
Email information@historic.org.nz
Website www.historic.org.nz
Items on contemporary heritage matters and issues. A preliminary letter to the editor is advisable.

Hospitality magazine
P.O. Box 9596, Newmarket, Auckland. Tel (09) 529 3000 Fax (09) 529 3001
Trade magazine for members of the hospitality industry (e.g., restaurateurs, hoteliers). Monthly.

IHC Community Moves
P.O. Box 4155, Wellington. Tel (04) 472 2247 Fax (04) 472 0429
Email community.moves@ihc.org.nz
Website www.ihc.org.nz
Free magazine for IHC supporters featuring news and information

about IHC and people with an intellectual disability and relevant issues. Published February, June and October.

Info-Link
P.O. Box 99-915, Newmarket, Auckland.
Tel (09) 846 4068 Fax (09) 846 8742
Website www.info-link.co.nz
Published quarterly, *Info-Link* presents extensive reports on market share throughout New Zealand and the South Pacific.

Interior Details
Private Bag 99-915, Newmarket, Auckland.
Tel (09) 846 4068 Fax (09) 846 8742
Website www.agm.co.nz
Publication for people working in residential interior design. Emphasis is on kitchens and bathrooms, home furniture and furnishings, trends, colours, textures and shapes.

Investigate
P.O. Box 302-188, North Harbour, North Shore 0751.
Tel (09) 373 3676 Fax (09) 373 3667
Email debbie@investigatemagazinecom
Website www.investigatemagazine.com
Monthly publication, news and current affairs.

Kai Tiaki: Nursing New Zealand
P.O. Box 2128, Wellington. Tel (04) 494 6386 Fax (04) 382 9993
Email annem@nzno.org.nz or teresa@nzno.org.nz
Website www.nzno.org.nz
Issues and policy relating to nursing in New Zealand and the work of the New Zealand Nurses Association. Published 11 times a year.

Kiwi Rider magazine
P.O. Box 299, Kumeu, Auckland.
Tel (09) 416 5307 Fax (09) 416 5308
Email editor.kiwirider@xtra.co.nz
Motorcycling news, features of interest to motorcycle owners, human interest stories with a riding theme, product reviews, etc. Sometimes uses freelance articles on events and personalities. A preliminary letter is desirable.

Landfall
P.O. Box 56, Dunedin. Tel (03) 479 8807 Fax (03) 479 8385
Email landfall@otago.co.nz
Landfall features New Zealand fiction and verse, critical work, commentaries, reviews, art and essays. Contributions are welcome; a self addressed envelope should be enclosed for the return of submissions. Contributions are also received by email. Payment is at set rates for published contributions.

Illustrated in both colour and monochrome, *Landfall* is published twice a year, in May and November.

Landscape New Zealand
Private Bag 99-915, Newmarket, Auckland.
Tel (09) 846 4068 Fax (09) 846 8742
Website www.agm.co.nz
Official journal of NZILA and LIANZ. Information on planning, design, construction and management of the landscape process for architects, designers and planners, as well as engineers, contractors and suppliers to the industry. Published bimonthly.

LawTalk
P.O. Box 5041, Wellington.
Tel (04) 472 7837 Fax (04) 473 7909
Email lawtalk@lawyers.co.nz
Website www.lawsoc.org.nz
Informed comment on legal issues.

Little Treasures
Private Bag 92-512, Wellesley St, Auckland 1141.
Tel (09) 308 2790 Fax (09) 379 2300
Email treasures@acpmagazines.co.nz
Website www.treasures.co.nz
Little Treasures offers information, support and affirmation to parents of preschool children. Articles relating to babies and small children, parenting and family life are relevant. The editor often uses articles from outside contributors. The style and tone of contributions should be warm and friendly, not judgmental in any way, or too authoritative. Contact with the editor should be made via email in the first instance. Bimonthly.

Mana
P.O. Box 108-233, Auckland. Tel (09) 358 0393 Fax (09) 358 0394
Website www.manaonline.co.nz
Mana is a monthly Maori magazine for all New Zealanders, and as such publishes anything relevant to Maori. Articles on art, politics, sport or fiction are welcomed. A preliminary letter to the associate editor is appreciated.

Management
P.O. Box 5544, Wellesley St, Auckland.
Tel (09) 630 9624 Fax (09) 630 5455
Email editor@management.co.nz
Website www.management.co.nz
Management usually uses commissioned articles, focusing on management techniques and innovations, particularly in a New Zealand context. It also has short news features and items of interest to people in business.

Twice a year (June and October) features *Management Women* insert. Black and white or colour illustrations are desirable. Payment is at the editor's discretion, and is negotiable, according to the size and worth of articles.

Marist Messenger
88 Hobson Street, Wellington 6001. Tel (04) 499 6546 Fax (04) 473 9423
Website www.maristmessenger.co.nz
A Roman Catholic monthly, founded in 1929, published by the Marist Fathers, which features devotional articles and articles on New Zealand Catholic history. Articles up to 1200 words. Payment is $20 a page.

Metro
Private Bag 92-512, Wellesley Street, Auckland 1141.
Tel (09) 308 2711 Fax (09) 379 2300
Email metro@acpmagazines.co.nz
Website www.metrolive.co.nz
Metro is a monthly New Zealand-wide magazine — but its focus is tightly on Auckland and the people who live there. Articles relevant to that audience will always be considered. Although a lot of the magazine's material is written by staff writers or commissioned from freelance writers with a track record, other outside contributions are sometimes used. Areas on which the magazine focuses include lifestyle, investigative pieces, articles about Auckland events and happenings, social issues, and general interest pieces of all sorts. The magazine's style is lively and informative.

Nelson Marlborough West Coast Tourist Times
P.O. Box 90, Belfast 8030, Christchurch. Tel (03) 323 7019 Fax (03) 323 7029
Email touristtimes@xtra.co.nz
Website www.touristtimes.co.nz
Monthly news and information on people, places and events in the Nelson, Marlborough, West Coast region, aimed mostly at tourists and visitors to the area. Seldom uses freelancers.

NetGuide
P.O. Box 92-512, Wellesley Street, Auckland 1141.
Tel (09) 366 9982 Fax (09) 308 2765
Email netguide@acpmagazines.co.nz
Website www.netguide.co.nz
Aimed at the New Zealand Internet user both at work and at home. It carries a well-balanced mix of feature articles, tutorials, reviews and guidelines for both the newcomer and more experienced user. Published monthly.

New Zealand New Idea
P.O. Box 1467, Auckland. Tel (09) 979 2700 Fax (09) 979 2721
Email brenda@pacificmagazines.co.nz
A large-circulation weekly featuring newsworthy, high-profile articles on lifestyles, personalities and other women's interest issues. Most features are

written by staff writers, but there is some scope for the freelancer to suggest ideas and articles to the editor.

New Zealand Adventure
P.O. Box 562, Whangaparaoa. Tel (09) 428 2441
Email p.media@xtra.co.nz
Website www.pacificmedia.co.nz
Adventure pursuits, personalities, equipment, places to explore.

New Zealand Author
P.O. Box 67-013, Mount Eden, Auckland 1349.
Tel (09) 379 4801 Fax (09) 379 4801
Email office@nzauthors.org.nz
Website www.authors.org.nz
The bimonthly newsletter of NZSA (formerly PEN) focuses on issues, news and events pertinent to New Zealand writing. The newsletter is free to members; others may subscribe. It welcomes press releases and images of member writers and is open to contributions from or about non-members. Payment is by negotiation.

New Zealand Autocar
P.O. Box 12-419, Penrose, Auckland. Tel (09) 573 3025 Fax (09) 573 3024
Email info@autocar.co.nz
Website www.fairfax.co.nz
A monthly publication for the motoring enthusiast, featuring new car releases, comparison tests, local and international industry news, articles on motorbikes, car audio, 4WD vehicles and model cars, Formula One, Indy and other motorsport.

New Zealand Baptist
P.O. Box 5, Beachlands, Auckland. Tel (09) 536 5715 Fax (09) 536 5714
Email editor@baptist.org.nz
Website www.baptist.org.nz
Family reading, reflecting the views and policies of the New Zealand Baptist Church. Human interest stories, news and comment.

New Zealand Bloodhorse
P.O. Box 272-1316, Papakura, Auckland. Tel (09) 269 2264
Email saskia@nzbloodhorse.co.nz
News and human interest stories concerning the thoroughbred racehorse, breeders, owners, trainers, jockeys.

New Zealand Books
Navigate House Level 7, 69 Boulcott St, Wellington.
Tel (04) 499 1569 Fax (04) 499 1424
Email jane_westway@xtra.co.nz
Website www.bookcouncil.org.nz

A review journal, which appears five times a year and concentrates exclusively on New Zealand publications.

New Zealand Bride and Groom
P.O. Box 37-356, Parnell, Auckland.
Tel (09) 336 1188 Fax (09) 373 5647
Email editorial@brideandgroom.co.nz
www.brideandgroom.co.nz
Quarterly magazine focusing on weddings and marriage with bridal fashion, wedding trends and honeymoon ideas.

New Zealand Business
P.O. Box 65-092, Mairangi Bay, Auckland.
Tel (09) 478 4771 Fax (09) 478 4779
Email editor@nzbusiness.co.nz
Website www.nzbusiness.co.nz
New Zealand Business has several features each month on business trends and techniques in New Zealand, successful companies and their strategies, and items of general interest to the professional manager and business people. Most articles are commissioned but there are openings for freelancers with a good idea. Contact the editor in the first instance.

NZ Catholic
P.O. Box 147-000, Ponsonby, Auckland.
Tel (09) 376 3067 Fax (09) 360 3065
Website www.nzcatholic.org.nz
New Zealand Catholic is a fortnightly national Catholic newspaper with a strong emphasis on news, both national and international. It is a tabloid-sized paper with wide appeal: accurate, balanced, up to date, stimulating and enjoyable, with high professional standards and attractive presentation.

New Zealand Classic Car
P.O. Box 46-020, Herne Bay, Auckland. Tel (09) 360 1480 Fax (09) 360 1470
Email qvincent@parkside.co.nz
Website www.classic-car.co.nz
Glossy, full-colour classic car magazine.

New Zealand Dairy Exporter
P.O. Box 5544, Wellesley St, Auckland.
Tel (09) 630 1624 x 328 Fax (09) 630 1046
Email glenys@dairymag.co.nz
Website www.dairymag.co.nz
A monthly publication, the *Dairy Exporter* is New Zealand's leading dairy farming journal, with stories on farm production, research, manufacturing and marketing. Informed comment (letters and articles) will be considered for publication. Submitted articles will be considered for Cow's Life, which includes light-hearted pieces with a dairying theme.

New Zealand Doctor
P.O. Box 31-348, Milford, Auckland.
Tel (09) 488 4266 Fax (09) 488 4284
Email editor@nzdoctor.co.nz
Website www.nzdoctor.co.nz
Medical issues.

New Zealand Education Review
P.O. Box 200, Wellington. Tel (04) 915 9795 Fax (04) 471 1080
Email editor@educationreview.co.nz
Website www.educationreview.co.nz
Provides national news coverage, features, opinion and analysis of the politics and issues of education. Published weekly.

NZEI Rourou
P.O. Box 466, Wellington. Tel (04) 384 9689 Fax (04) 385 1772
Website www.nzei.org.nz/rourou/rourou.htm
The magazine of the New Zealand Educational Institute, published 12 times a year and distributed to 40,000 NZEI members and educational organisations. Featuring articles on educational, social, industrial and political developments, research and innovations, covering news from local, national and international angles. Full colour.
Letters to the editor and unsolicited freelance articles and/or photos accepted but usually not paid. Contact the editor to discuss submissions.

New Zealand Fishing News
P.O. Box 12-965, Penrose, Auckland. Tel (09) 634 1800 Fax (09) 634 2948
Email grant.dixon@fishnz.co.nz
Website www.fishnz.co.nz
New Zealand Fishing News is aimed at people who fish for sport, and as such is willing to consider articles about freshwater and saltwater fishing, rock fishing, beach fishing, boat fishing and big-game fishing. Articles generally have a 'newsy' flavour to them that offers the reader information they can use to improve their own results. Freelance contributions are welcome but preliminary contact with the editor to discuss content is appreciated. Monthly.

New Zealand Fitness
P.O. Box 105-483. Auckland. Tel (09) 366 0404 Fax (09) 366 0402
New Zealand's only fitness magazine. Articles on exercise, motivation, medicine and rehabilitation, fitness fashion, nutrition, inspiration and endurance. Bimonthly.

New Zealand 4WD and Sports Vehicles
P.O. Box 65-092, Mairangi Bay, Auckland.
Tel (09) 478 4771 Fax (09) 478 4779
Email cathy@adrenalin.co.nz
Website www.nz4wd.co.nz

Monthly publication, covers a range of topics of interest to the 4WD vehicle buyer and driver.

New Zealand Gardener
P.O. Box 6341, Wellesley Street, Auckland.
Tel (09) 353 1010 Fax (09) 353 1020
Email lynda.hallinarh@nzgardener.co.nz
Website www.fairfax.co.nz
New Zealand's largest monthly magazine for gardening enthusiasts, full of news, features, plant profiles, design ideas, tips and other items of interest to gardeners. Some opportunities for freelance writers who know their subject; high quality colour transparencies may well assist in selecting successful articles. Preliminary letter to the editor regarding content advisable before submitting freelance material.

New Zealand Genealogist
P.O. Box 5523, Moray Place, Dunedin.
Tel (09) 570 4248 Fax (09) 570 4238
Email tarting@deepsouth.co.nz
Website www.geneology.org.nz
Interesting articles about family research, techniques, tips, etc., for amateur researchers.

New Zealand Geographic
P.O. Box 3855, Auckland. Tel (09) 307 0399 Fax (09) 303 0127
Email warren@nzgeographic.co.nz
Website www.nzgeographic.co.nz
A bimonthly full-colour magazine with a wide range of articles on New Zealand geography, history, culture, natural history, environment, industry, recreation, science and exploration aimed at the intelligent general reader. The magazine seeks contributions, but it is suggested that prospective writers should carefully study its style before they submit material and contact the editor before they embark on possible stories. Payment for features is negotiable with the editor; good quality transparencies, colour prints and black and white shots are paid for separately.

New Zealand Growing Today
P.O. Box 12-965, Penrose, Auckland. Tel (09) 634 1800 Fax (09) 634 2948
Email nadine.hall@growing-today.co.nz
Website www.fairfax.co.nz
How-to-do-it information on horticulture, agriculture and lifestyle blocks. Monthly.

New Zealand Home and Entertaining
Private Bag 92-512, Wellesley Street, Auckland 1141.
Tel (09) 308 2845 Fax (09) 379 2300
Email homeent@acpmagazines.co.nz

Website www.acpmedia.co.nz
Bimonthly publication with a focus on New Zealand's leading-edge, contemporary architecture and design. Also quick, smart recipes for the busy professional.

New Zealand Horse and Pony
P.O. Box 12-965, Penrose, Auckland.
Tel (09) 634 1800 Fax (09) 634 2948
Email rowan.dixon@horse-pony.co.nz
Website www.horse-pony.co.nz
Covers all disciplines (except Western) regularly. Instruction, veterinary, horsemastership, etc., major event reports. No fiction. Full colour. Published monthly. Contact editor initially re freelance submissions.

New Zealand House and Garden
P.O. Box 6341, Wellesley Street, Auckland.
Tel (09) 353 1010 Fax (09) 353 1020
Email wendy.barnard@nzhouse-garden.co.nz
Website www.nzhouseandgarden
Monthly magazine focusing on New Zealand homes, style and design, also food, travel and design trends. Most features are commissioned. Contact editor first before making submissions.

New Zealand International Review
New Zealand Institute of International Affairs,
c/o Victoria University of Wellington, P. O. Box 600, Wellington.
Tel (04) 463 5356
Email ian.mcgibbon@mch.govt.nz
Website www.arts.auckland.ac.nz
International relations generally and with particular reference to New Zealand and the South Pacific. Freelance submissions of not more than 3000 words are welcome. No payments are made for articles published in the magazine.

New Zealand Journal of Sports Medicine
P.O. Box 6398, Dunedin.
Tel (03) 477 7887 Fax (03) 477 7882
Email smnznat@xtra.co.nz
Website www.sportsmedicine.co.nz
Material relevant to sports medicine and related disciplines.

New Zealand Kennel Gazette
c/o New Zealand Kennel Club, Private Bag 50903, Porirua 6220, Wellington.
Tel (04) 237 4489 Fax (04) 237 0721
Email gazette@nzkc.org.nz
Website www.nzkc.org.nz
Features relating to dogs and their breeding.

New Zealand Life and Leisure
P.O. Box 109-688, Newmarket, Auckland.
Tel (09) 529 5941 Fax (09) 529 5942
Email kate@nzlifeandleisure.co.nz
Website www.nzlifeandleisure.co.nz
Bimonthly lifestyle magazine with profiles of talented New Zealanders, food, domestic travel, fashion and beauty. Top quality photography. Most material commissioned. Contact the editor before making a submission.

NZ Lifestyle Block
P.O. 92-512, Wellesley St, Auckland 1141. Tel (09) 308 2833
Email nzlsb@tradergroup.co.nz
Website www.lifestyleblock.co.nz
Informative, entertaining and practical guide to lifestyle farming.

New Zealand Lifestyle Farmer
P.O. Box 4233, Auckland. Tel (09) 523 5056 Fax (09) 524 1170
Email lifestylefarmer.nz@ruralpress.com
Website http//lifestylefarmerfarmonline.co.nz
Monthly magazine for lifestyle farmers offering practical advice and information on animal care, growing plants, machine maintenance, etc.

New Zealand Listener
P.O. Box 90-783, Auckland Mail Centre.
Tel (09) 373 9400 Fax (09) 326 6941
Email submissions@listener.co.nz
Website www.listener.co.nz
The *Listener*, established in 1939, is New Zealand's only national weekly current affairs and entertainment magazine, featuring a wide range of articles on lifestyle, current events, topics of general interest to New Zealanders, comment, opinion, political issues, short stories, poetry, reviews and regular columns. Unsolicited contributions and story ideas are welcome, either in printed form or by email.

NZ Marketing Magazine
P.O. Box 5544, Wellesley Street, Auckland.
Tel (09) 630 1624 x 312 Fax (09) 630 1046
Email graham@marketingmag.co.nz
Website www.marketingmag.co,nz
A monthly magazine for marketing and advertising professionals, *Marketing* employs a readable style to get across features about sales and management techniques, New Zealand success (and failure) stories, marketing news and information, comment, opinion and political assessments. Regular columns include travel, book reviews, international news and short articles of interest to marketing people. The magazine generally uses staff writers or commissions material from people in the marketing world — however, there is opportunity for contributions from writers with a

particular angle or knowledge of marketing. A preliminary letter to the editor is not essential.

New Zealand Outdoor
P.O. Box 13-370, Tauranga. Tel (07) 541 3553 Fax (07) 541 3223
Email info@nzoutdoor
Website www.nzoutdoor.co.nz
A bimonthly magazine catering to hunters and fishermen, *New Zealand Outdoor* requires factual, practical articles on these subjects, and technical pieces on equipment, etc. Payment is by arrangement. Photographs and illustrations are welcomed.

New Zealand PC World
P.O. Box 6813, Wellesley Street, Auckland.
Tel (09) 302 5720 Fax (09) 377 4604
Website www.pcworld.co.nz
News, information and tips for users of PCs, published in glossy format every month. Some potential here for knowledgeable freelancers.

New Zealand Pharmacy
P.O. Box 33-146, Takapuna, Auckland. Tel (09) 486 0077
Email rlehdof@hayleymedia.com
Website www.pharmacyjournal.co.nz
Magazine distributed to pharmacists throughout New Zealand.

The New Zealand Plumber's Journal
P.O. Box 1531, Nelson. Tel (03) 548 2408
Email fabnelson@xtra.co.nz
Plumbing materials, equipment and projects, gasfitting, drainlaying, roofing, solar and associated trades, business issues and health and safety issues. Bimonthly. Editor always seeking articles of interest to plumbers and the plumbing trade.

New Zealand Printer
P.O. Box 39-523, Howick, Auckland.
Tel (09) 271 6274 Fax (09) 271 6272
Email editorial@i-grafix.com
Website www.i-grafix.com
News, features and information for those involved in the New Zealand printing industry.

New Zealand Professional Skipper
4 Prince Regent Drive, Half Moon Bay, Manukau City.
Tel (09) 533 4336 Fax (09) 533 4337
Email keith@skipper.co.nz
Website www.skipper.co.nz
A bimonthly magazine for professional boat operators, featuring both

professional and lifestyle articles on commercial boat activities and marine tourism and adventure. The magazine occasionally accepts unsolicited submissions from freelancers, although the editor prefers to be contacted in advance to discuss article focus and the rate of pay. All articles should be no longer than 2000 words and supported with colour photographs.

New Zealand Retail
P.O. Box 12-086, Wellington. Tel (04) 472 3733 Fax (04) 472 1071
Email nzretail@retail.org.nz
Website www.retail.org.nz
New Zealand Retail is a monthly business magazine. It publishes commissioned articles written by experienced journalists and is prepared to discuss potential articles on topics relevant to the industry. All articles should offer retailers a way to improve the profitability of their businesses. Advertorial is never accepted.

New Zealand Rugby World
P.O. Box 78-070, Auckland. Tel (09) 360 5700 Fax (09) 360 5702
Email editor@nzrugbyworld.com
Website www.nzrugbyworld.com
Rugby magazine covering national and international events.

New Zealand Ski and Snow
P.O. Box 562, Whangaparaoa. Tel (09) 428 2441 Fax (09) 428 2443
Email p.media@xtra.co.nz
Website www.pacificmedia.co.nz
Skiing, snowboarding, personalities, après ski, places to stay and visit.

New Zealand Skier
37 Murphy Rd, Gisborne. Tel (06) 868 7974 Fax (09) 868 7971
Email hq@ohanamedia.co.nz
Website www.nzsnowboarder.nzl.com/ohana.html
A full-colour glossy published twice during winter in June and August, the magazine features equipment reports, articles on skiing destinations and expeditions, personality profiles and news and information of interest to New Zealand skiers. A preliminary letter to the editor is advisable.

New Zealand Snowboarder Magazine
37 Murphy Rd, Gisborne. Tel (06) 868 7974 Fax (09) 868 7971
Email hq@nzsnowboarder.nzl.com
Webiste www.nzsnowboarder.nzl.com
Published each May, July, September, covering all aspects of New Zealand snowboarding. Freelance editorial and photographic submissions considered. Also publishes New Zealand Skateboarder.

New Zealand Surfing Magazine
P.O. Box 14-109, Panmure, Auckland. Tel (09) 570 2658 Fax (09) 570 2684

Email surfedit@surfingnz.com
Website www.surfingnz.com
A large-circulation magazine, published every two months for surfing enthusiasts, *Surfing* is always on the lookout for good feature articles about surfing events, exploits, personalities and places.

New Zealand Today
P.O. Box 8673, Symonds St, Auckland. Tel (09) 369 5412
Email editor@nztoday.co.nz
Website www.drivermagazine.co.nz
Bimonthly travel/lifestyle magazine.

New Zealand Tree Grower
P.O. Box 2002, Wellington. Tel (04) 427 0432 Fax (04) 473 6904
Email nzffa@clear.net.nz
Website www.nzffa.org.nz
Quarterly publication distributed to all members of New Zealand Farm and Forestry Association and subscribers. Contains information for anyone interested in growing trees.

New Zealand Trucking
P.O. Box 12-965, Penrose, Auckland. Tel (09) 634 1800 Fax (09) 634 5600
Email editor@nztrucking.co.nz
Website www.fairfax.co.nz
Heavy vehicle features, aimed at enthusiasts. Events, places, personalities, new equipment, trucks.

New Zealand Truck and Driver
P.O. Box 112-062, Auckland. Tel (09) 571 3544 Fax (09) 571 3549
Email dave@trucker.co.nz
Website www.truckanddriver.co.nz
Official magazine of the Road Transport Forum, delivered to every major transport fleet in New Zealand.Trucks and transport.

New Zealand Weddings
P.O. Box 1467, Auckland. Tel (09) 979 2700 Fax (09) 979 2723
Email katy.paterson@pacificmagazines.co.nz
Website www.newzealandweddings.co.nz
NZ Weddings is published three times a year, targeting the 20,000 NZ couples who are married every year. It is every bride's essential guide to getting married, covering topics from hair and beauty to gowns, locations and planning advice. The editor is open to submissions of stories and photographs.

New Zealand Woman's Day
Private Bag 92-512, Wellesley Street, Auckland. Tel (09) 308 2700
Email wdaynz@acpmagazines.co.nz

Website www.acpmedia.co.nz
Items of interest to women throughout New Zealand feature in this New Zealand edition of the Australian mass market weekly. International and local gossip, lifestyle, personalities, events and general interest pieces — all with a strong human interest angle to them. The editor is on the lookout for good ideas, and articles should be between 1000 and 1500 words. Photographs are a feature of nearly every article. These can be supplied by writers, if they are competent photographers. Contact the editor first. Payment is by agreement with the editor.

New Zealand Woman's Weekly
P.O. Box 90-119, Auckland Mail Centre, Auckland.
Tel (09) 373 9400 Fax 373 9405
Email editor@nww.co.nz
Website www.nzww.co.nz
The magazine uses articles from outside contributors fairly frequently, but only about five per cent of the total submitted material is used, for a variety of reasons. Often the editor will commission a writer who has written for the magazine before. Feature articles, on topics such as human interest stories, news backgrounders and 'newsy' personality profiles, should be between 1000 and 2000 words in length; articles should be accompanied by colour transparencies or colour prints if possible. The *Woman's Weekly* has staff photographers in the main centres and some provincial areas, who are able to illustrate contributed articles if necessary. Many articles fail because the illustrations and photographs that accompany them are of poor quality. Contact the editor first.

Next
Private Bag 92-512, Auckland. Tel (09) 308 2797
Email next@acpmagazines.co.nz
Website www.acpmedia.co.nz
A glossy magazine for women with general interest features, profiles and informative articles. Published monthly.

North and South
Private Bag 92-152, Wellesley Street, Auckland.
Tel (09) 308 2754
Email northsouth@acpmagazines.co.nz
North and South is published monthly. The editor welcomes 600- to 1000-word community-based articles on interesting people, places and events. Positive, good news stories are particularly welcome. For longer features a 400-word story précis is required by the editor, so an article of 4000 to 7000 words can then be commissioned. If writers are also competent photographers, they can submit colour transparencies with feature articles; high quality prints are sometimes acceptable. Where freelance contributors are not comfortable with taking their own photographs, North and South will organise its own photographers to illustrate stories.

On Arts
Creative New Zealand, P.O. Box 3806, Wellington.
Tel (04) 473 0880 Fax (04) 471 2865
Email ionam@creativenz.govt.nz
Website www.creativenz.govt.nz
Art and events in New Zealand. Published three times a year by Creative New Zealand.

Out!
Private Bag 92-126, Auckland. Tel (09) 377 9031
Email outnz@xtra.co.nz
Website www.out.co.nz
Gay magazine, featuring articles on social and homosexual issues, lifestyles, etc. A preliminary letter to the editor is not always necessary; payment is by arrangement.

Pacific Wings
P.O. Box 39-099, Harewood, Christchurch. Tel (03) 359 0256
Email info@nzwings.co.nz
Website www.nzwings.co.nz
Aviation.

Pet New Zealand
P.O. Box 37-356, Parnell, Auckland.
Tel (09) 336 1188 Fax (09) 336 1189
Email enquiries@petmag.co.nz
Website www.petmag.co.nz
Quarterly magazine for animal lovers.

Pharmacy Today
P.O. Box 31-348, Milford, Auckland. Tel (09) 488 4290 Fax (09) 489 6240
Email jhoyle@pharmacy-today.co.nz
Website www.pharmacy-today.co.nz
Pharmacy news and developments relating to new products, retailing and political news.

Playmarket News
P.O. Box 9767, Te Aro, Wellington. Tel (04) 382 8462 Fax (04) 382 8461
Email info@playmarket.org.nz
Website www.playmarket.org.nz
A quarterly magazine which spotlights successful Kiwi playwrights, provides general news and related articles, and highlights productions at leading New Zealand venues.

Player
Private Bag 37-745, Auckland. Tel (09) 302 6191 Fax (09) 377 2115
Email player@armadapublishing.co.nz

Website www.playermagazine.co.nz
In depth interviews and profiles with expert analysis of sporting issues.

Plenty
P.O. Box 91-344, AMSC, Auckland. Tel (09) 360 6424 Fax (09) 358 7291
Email john@jonespublishing.co.nz
Website www.jonespublishing.co.nz
Quarterly publication aimed at active over-fifty-year-olds, with features, profiles and articles of interest.

Positive Living
P.O. Box 10-688, Wellington 6143. Tel (04) 801 9338 Fax (04) 801 9338
Email information@ageconcern.org.nz
Website www.ageconcern.org.nz
Age Concern's bimonthly publication has a committed readership from the 50-plus age group, with feature articles targeted at readers who are 80-plus. It is widely read by caregivers and relatives and keeps in touch with matters affecting the older generation. The editor will occasionally pay for freelance articles, but generally receives more than enough Age Concern-related information and contributions from older people. Prospective contributors should contact the editor in advance.

PPTA News
P.O. Box 2119, Wellington. Tel (04) 384 9964 Fax (04) 382 8763
Email enquiries@ppta.org.nz
Website www.ppta.org.nz
The *PPTA News* is the official publication of the Post Primary Teachers' Association, and is published eleven times a year. Preliminary contact with the editor is advisable — the *PPTA News* welcomes contributions of between 500 and 600 words in the areas of educational developments, informed opinion, book reviews and some poetry. Colour prints, cartoons and line drawings are used to illustrate articles.

Prime Times
P. O. Box 562, Whangaparoa, Auckland.
Tel (09) 428 2441 Fax (09) 428 2443
Email p.media@xtra.co.nz
Website www.pacificmedia.co.nz
Children's magazine aimed at 8–13 year olds.

Principals Today
P. O. Box 1879, Christchurch. Tel (03) 961 5098 Fax (03) 961 5091
Email editor@academy.net.nz
Website www.acadamey.net.nz
Principals Today is directed at the education sector and reaches schools throughout the country at the beginning of each school term. Its wide range of informative topics and in-depth analysis of the issues that matter has

earned it the reputation of being an important 'tool' for principals, teachers and boards of trustees. News and views are paramount — so too are features which assist education decision makers. Some columns. The editor is willing to consider good, well-written articles.

Prodesign
Private Bag 99-915, Newmarket, Auckland. Tel (09) 846 2722 x 323
Email vicki.poland@agm.co.nz
Website www.agm.co.nz
Official journal of the Designers' Institute of New Zealand. Serves the key design disciplines: interior, graphics and product. Bimonthly.

Progressive Building
Private Bag 99-915, Newmarket, Auckland. Tel (09) 846 2722 x 326
Email lisavb@agm.co.nz
Website www.agm.co.nz
Official journal of the New Zealand Institute of Building. Bimonthly which addresses the needs of both large construction companies and small independent builders and contractors.

Pulp
P.O. Box 8461, Auckland. Tel (09) 300 4444 Fax (09) 303 0212
Email editor@pulpmagazine.co.nz
Website www.pulp.co.nz
Street fashion culture for 15–35 year olds. Fashion, beauty, movies, music, celebrity gossip.

Reader's Digest
Email melissa.haywood@readersdigest.com
Website www.readersdigest.co.nz
Human interest stories are the mainstay of this international monthly publication. Almost all the articles are written by freelance writers — however, the New Zealand edition is largely made up of contributions from overseas editions, and is compiled in Australia. The editor is always willing to consider good, strong stories about personal experiences and challenges; articles should always have a positive, interesting tone, and should be under 5000 words. There are several regular sections for short anecdotes, for which there is a payment; payment rates for longer features are very high. A preliminary email is advisable to ascertain whether an article will be suitable for publication in *Reader's Digest*; photographs, where necessary, should be submitted with material.

Real Groove
P.O. Box 91-285, Auckland. Tel (09) 302 3940 Fax (09) 302 3955
Email editor@realgroovy.co.nz
Monthly music magazine which regularly uses freelancers. Film, DVD, book video game news and reviews. Contact the editor first regarding submissions.

Rip It Up
P.O. Box 90-736, Auckland. Tel (09) 921 0836 Fax (09) 623 8261
Email info@ripituponline.com
Website www.ripituponline.com
Rip It Up is distributed nationwide and is aimed at rock music fans of all ages, with an interest in intelligent, informative features and reviews of New Zealand and international music. Much material is commissioned or written by staff writers; there is, however, always scope for the good freelancer to have material accepted. Prospective writers should study the magazine carefully, to get some feel for the style and level of *Rip It Up*. A preliminary letter to the editor is always a good idea; photographs, in black and white or colour, are also desirable.

Rod and Rifle
P.O. Box 38-138, Petone, Wellington. Tel (04) 569 3198 Fax (04) 569 1138
Email enquiries@rodandrifle.co.nz
Website www.rodandrifle.co.nz
Hunting, fishing and other outdoor pursuits are featured in this magazine. Practical articles on aspects of these pursuits are welcome; technical articles on equipment are used; reviews of events, people and places also feature. A preliminary letter to the editor is not necessary, but close study of the magazine is recommended. Black and white or colour photographs should accompany articles where possible. Bimonthly.

Rugby News
P.O. Box 11-553, Ellerslie, Auckland. Tel (09) 525 5434 Fax (09) 525 5435
Email news@rugby.co.nz
Website www.rugby.co.nz
Weeky magazine delivering comprehensive coverage of domestic and international rugby. Match reports, player features, including Super 14, All Blacks, Air NZ Cup and club and grass roots coverage. Thirty-six editions published in-season.

Rural News
Rural News Group Ltd, P. O. Box 3855, Auckland 1.
Tel (09) 307 0399 Fax (09) 307 0122
Email editor@ruralnews.co.nz
Website www.ruralnews.co.nz
Publishers of agribusiness newspapers *Rural News* and *Dairying Today*, fortnightly and monthly respectively. Main focus is international and national hard news on the business and politics of agriculture, with some features on farm management, personality profiles and animal health issues. Uses freelance material if tightly written and topical. Good photographs also welcome. Submissions should be directed to the editor.

School Journal
Learning Media, P.O. Box 3293, Wellington.

Tel (04) 472 5522 Fax (04) 472 6444
Email schooljournal@learningmedia.co.nz
Website www.learningmedia.co.nz
Chances are, if you've attended a New Zealand school in the last eighty years, you will have read a *School Journal* at some time. Published regularly at four different reading levels, the *School Journal* features New Zealand fiction, non-fiction, poetry and drama for children. Much of the material used in the Journal is submitted by freelance writers; the editors are constantly on the lookout for high quality material which will stimulate children from the ages of seven to 13. All submissions are acknowledged promptly, but assessment of each manuscript can take some time, due to the volume received. Poems, articles, stories and plays between 300 and 1000 words are preferred, depending on the level of the intended audience. No preliminary letter is needed. In addition to the *School Journal,* several other series of children's fiction and non-fiction are produced by Learning Media. Pieces in Maori and Pacific Island languages are welcome.

Simply You
P.O. Box 137-223, Parnell, Auckland. Tel (09) 377 2200
Email julie@simplyyou.co.nz
Website www.simplyyou.co.nz
Biannual style guide with fashion, beauty, in-season trends and how-to advice. Also *Simply You – Living,* a biannual interior design magazine. Most of the features are written in-house or by a staff of regular contributors. Check with the editor before submitting material.

Takahe Magazine
P.O. Box 13-335, Christchurch 8001.
Email markj07@ibm.net
A quarterly magazine which publishes short stories and poetry by new and established authors. A grant from Creative New Zealand has made possible a small payment for each item published. Submissions on disk are appreciated but not essential. Remember SAE for a reply.

Taste
Private Bag 52-512, Wellesley St, Auckland. Tel (09) 308 2403
Email taste@acpmagazines.co.nz
Website www.taste.co.nz
Monthly food magazine featuring one hundred-plus recipes, meal ideas, wine tasting, etc. Mainly written by a stable of regular contributors.

Tearaway Magazine, Tearaway Glue, Tearaway Teacher Resource, Tearaway Online
P.O. Box 473, 31A Taupo Quay, Wanganui.
Tel (06) 349 0049 Fax (06) 345 8881
Email online editor: tristan@tearaway.co.nz or
magazine editor: arena@tearaway.co.nz

Website www.tearaway.co.nz
Tearaway is NZ's biggest youth publication for the 10-plus age group. It targets 13-19 year-olds and is distributed through secondary schools nationwide during term time and McDonalds restaurants during holidays and is available throughout the year at selected 'street' outlets, public libraries, and movie theatres. Not a cover price magazine. *Tearaway* is written by young people for young people, and provides good quality, credible entertainment and infotainment — life skills, music, fashion, sport, creative writing, etc. Some freelance contributions are accepted. A letter to the editor outlining your ideas is preferred.

That's Life!
P.O. Box 1467, Auckland. Tel (09) 979 2700 Fax (09) 979 2721
Email thatslife@pacpubs.com.au
Website www.pacpubs.com.au
Lifestyle magazine with unusual human interest stories, mainly supplied from Australia.

Trends
Trends Publishing International publishes: *New Home Trends, Interior Trends, Bathroom Trends, Kitchen Trends, Outdoor Living* and *Holiday Home Trends, Architecture & Design Trends, Renovation Trends*.
P.O. Box 11-908, Ellerslie, Auckland. Tel (09) 571 5700 Fax (09) 571 5703
Email reception@trendsideas.com
Website www.trendsideas.com
Trends is a glossy architectural reference publication for homeowners, architects and industry professionals. It is published internationally, including 15 editions per year in New Zealand. Each edition has a focus on a particular part of the home or commercial industry, with property features, as well as a showcase on new products, retailers and manufacturers. All articles are written in-house and regular freelance photographers are used. As well as print media, Trends Publishing also specialises in online and television media.

TV Guide
P.O. Box 1327, Auckland. Tel (09) 302 1300 Fax (09) 373 3036
Email editor@tv-guide.co.nz
Website www.fairfaxnz.co.nz
Television-related articles and television guide.

Unlimited
P.O. Box 6813, Wellesley Street, Auckland.
Tel (09) 375 6023 Fax (09) 377 4604
Email editor@unlimited.net.nz
Website www.unlimited.co.nz
Unlimited is New Zealand's leading business magazine. Three times awarded business magazine of the year, it has collected 28 journalism and design

awards. *Unlimited* is owned by IDG Communications, one of the world's largest publishers, and specialises in covering New Zealand's knowledge economy.

Urbis
Private Bag 99-915, Newmarket, Auckland. Tel (09) 846 2722 x 321
Email melinda.williams@agm.co.nz
Website www.agm.co.nz
Houses, architecture and design, with features on architects, new technology and products. Bimonthly.

Urbis Landscapes
Private Bag 99-915, Newmarket, Auckland. Tel (09) 846 2722 x 320
Email tom.museth@agm.co.nz
Website www.agm.co.nz
Quarterly featuring designed landscapes, houses, buildings and spaces in between.

Weekend Gardener
P. O. Box 8185, Symonds Street, Auckland
Tel (09) 361 5512 Fax (09) 361 5512
Email wgpubs@xtra.co.nz
Website www.weekendgardener.co.nz
Weekend Gardener is New Zealand's fastest-growing gardening magazine. Published fortnightly, it has a do-it-yourself focus and aims to inspire and educate New Zealand gardeners with articles about local gardeners, garden design, plants, organics, edible gardening, and garden art. Freelance submissions, including colour transparencies, are welcomed by the editor. Email enquiries are preferred.

Your Home & Garden
Private Bag 92-512, Wellesley Street, Auckland. Tel (09) 308 2739
Email yhg@acpmagazines.co.nz
Website www.acpmedia.co.nz
Achievable, inspirational homes — full of budget-friendly ideas for renovating and decorating. Story ideas should be emailed to the editor first.

16 Book Publishers

Well over 300 organisations and companies publish material in any one year in New Zealand. Some, such as government departments and local bodies, are prolific; others, such as small private presses, may produce only one small book a year. Major commercial publishers average about 20 to 40 books per year.

Since the first edition of *The New Zealand Writer's Handbook,* there have been a lot of changes in the book publishing industry — rationalisations, mergers and sometimes closures. Fortunately, a lot of new companies have also sprung up. Authors should always check, by telephone, or by looking through bookshops, on the latest status of the publishing company they wish to approach. In the selective list that follows, the most likely publishers for New Zealand writers are given a detailed entry. Smaller publishers who specialise in New Zealand literature are also mentioned, as well as other companies that play a role in New Zealand publishing, such as distributors or agents. In addition, there are a few companies who specialise in 'book packaging' — preparing and publishing books that have been commissioned by a client.

The best way of deciding whether or not a company is right for your manuscript is to look through its books in a bookshop or library, contact the company for a copy of its catalogue, or have a look at its website (if it has one). This will give you a full idea of the material the company is interested in. It is a waste of time sending your novel to a company that only publishes reference books, or your latest collection of verse to a publisher that publishes no poetry. Most New Zealand companies specialise in one or more areas — gardening, natural history, children's books, educational texts, etc. — but some will publish something outside of their normal range if they consider it to be worthwhile.

For a comprehensive list of publishers, see the latest edition of *New Zealand Books in Print*, which includes an alphabetical directory in its final section. Regular insert sheets are also produced for this book, detailing changes in address or contact numbers. Your local library should have copies of updates as well as the book itself.

When approaching a publisher for the first time, a little homework beforehand is invaluable. Contact the publisher to see if they accept unsolicited material — and if they do, how they prefer to receive it: hard copy, disk, or email. Most publishers prefer a preliminary letter that outlines your work, or with perhaps a sample chapter — this is more likely to be read than an entire manuscript. Be prepared to wait up to a couple of months for a decision to be made. If you want your work back, send a stamped addressed envelope.

If your work is accepted, a publishing contract will be discussed (see Chapter 9). Reputable publishers will publish your work at their own expense. A 'vanity publisher', on the other hand, usually places advertisements that solicit manuscripts from writers. The writer then receives a very enthusiastic response full of flattering praise for the work. The catch is that the publisher wants a hefty fee for publishing the work. Although royalties on sales are sometimes promised, little attempt is made at promoting and marketing the book, except to offer the writer the opportunity of purchasing the books at a 'reduced price'. Writers should beware of vanity publishers.

Aoraki Press
P.O. Box 11-699, Wellington. Tel (04) 385 8528
Maori publications and Maori education.

Auckland University Press
University of Auckland, Private Bag 92-019, Auckland.
Tel (09) 373 7528 Fax (09) 373 7465
Email aup@auckland.ac.nz
Website www.auckland.ac.nz/aup
AUP publishes New Zealand history, art history, Maori and Pacific studies, books on contemporary issues, poetry and biography, in addition to scholarly and academic works.

Awa Press
P.O. Box 11-416, Manners St, Wellington.
Tel (04) 385 0740 Fax (04) 382 9032
Email info@awapress.co.nz
General market non-fiction.

David Bateman Ltd
P.O. Box 100-242, North Shore Mail Centre, Auckland 1330.
Tel (09) 415 7664 Fax (09) 415 8892
Email bateman@bateman.co.nz
Website www.bateman.co.nz
David Bateman Ltd is a general publisher with interests in art, reference, lifestyle, health, biography, cookery, natural history, history, gardening, outdoor pursuits, etc. Special interests include books developed and produced for the international market. The company produces 35–40 books a year for both domestic and international markets.

Boat Books
22 Westhaven Drive, Westhaven, Auckland.
Tel (09) 358 5691 Fax (09) 358 5817
Email crew@boatbooks.co.nz
Website www.boatbooks.co.nz
Technical and educational marine books, publishing as Captain Teach Press.

Bush Press Communications Ltd, publishing as The Bush Press of New Zealand
P.O. Box 33-029, Takapuna, Auckland 0740. Tel & Fax (09) 486 2667
Email bush.press@clear.net.nz
Bush Press specialises in the natural and historic heritage of New Zealand, but considers general books about New Zealand, outdoor books, guides, regional publications, photography, biography and books for visitors and children. Family and local histories, museum and travel guides, etc., are published by arrangement. Fiction is not wanted. Send an outline, sample chapters and a self-addressed envelope to establish possible interest.

Canterbury University Press
University of Canterbury, Private Bag 4800, Christchurch.
Tel (03) 364 2914 Fax (03) 364 2044
Email mail@cup.canterbury.ac.nz
Website www.cup.canterbury.ac.nz
A dual list of scholarly and general titles, particularly non-fiction.

Cape Catley Ltd
P.O. Box 32-622, Devonport. Tel & Fax (09) 445 9668
Email capecatley@xtra.co.nz
Cape Catley publishes New Zealand fiction, children's books, social justice, feminism, politics, local history, biography and autobiography, gardening and yachting. A preliminary letter is preferred rather than the whole manuscript. Decisions usually take a month.

CCH New Zealand
P.O. Box 2378, Auckland. Tel (09) 488 2760 Fax (09) 489 3312
Website www.cch.co.nz
CCH New Zealand is a specialist tax, business and legal publisher and is part of the Wolters Kluwer Group worldwide. The company produces up to 15 books per year in addition to its updating and electronic services. CCH New Zealand does not deal with or publish fiction.

Celebrity Books
P.O. Box 331-071, Takapuna, Auckland.
Tel (09) 442 1046 Fax (09) 414 2457
Email celebritybill@xtra.co.nz
Celebrity Books specialises in general interest, New Zealand history, sports and personality books. Fiction is not wanted. The company produces up to 10 books per year, mainly in New Zealand, with a small number published each year in Australia. A preliminary letter to the publisher is preferred, with decisions made within a month.

Darius Press Ltd
P.O. Box 4266, Wanganui. Tel (06) 348 4790 Fax (06) 348 4797
Fiction, non-fiction, poetry, storytelling with a commercial edge.

Dunmore Press Ltd
P.O. Box 25-080, Wellington. Tel (04) 472 2705 Fax (04) 471 0604
Email books@dunmore.co.nz
Website www.dunmore.co.nz
Dunmore Press is a prolific small publisher of about 25 general non-fiction titles per year including health, economics, politics, history and biography. Some are for the general trade, while other titles are intended for university, polytechnic and secondary school markets. Decisions are generally made within three to six weeks.

ESA Publications (NZ) Ltd
P.O. Box 9453, Newmarket, Auckland. Tel 0800 372 266 Fax 0800 329 372
Email info@esa.co.nz
ESA produces NCEA Study Guides, AME and StartRight and Workbooks covering a wide range of subjects for students in New Zealand primary and secondary schools.

Exisle Publishing
PO Box 60-490, Titirangi, Auckland.
Tel (09) 817 9192 Fax (09) 817 2295
www.exislepublishing.com

New Zealand and Australian based independent publisher with extensive international links. Areas include self-help and well-being, travel, Kiwi and Australian local interest, sports, biographies, history and adventure. Full submission guidelines on website. No electronic submissions.

Grantham House Publishing
P.O. Box 17-256, Wellington 6033.
Tel (04) 381 3071 Fax (04) 381 3067
Grantham House publishes general non-fiction with a New Zealand theme, particularly in the area of illustrated histories; it specialises in land, sea and air transportation. Grantham House also operates Bookprint Consultants Ltd.

Hachette Livre NZ Ltd
P.O. Box 100-749, North Shore Mail Centre, Auckland.
Tel (09) 478 1000 Fax (09) 478 1010
Email admin@hachette.co.nz
Hachette Livre is a publisher of New Zealand books for the general retail trade, concentrating on high-profile, non-fiction and brand publishing. They publish around 35 new titles a year. Material is acknowledged upon receipt.

Halcyon Publishing Ltd
P.O. Box 360, Auckland 1140. Tel (09) 489 5337 Fax (09) 489 5218
Email gurr@halcyonpublishing.co.nz
Halcyon's imprint, The Halcyon Press, concentrates mainly on outdoor sporting pursuits, including fishing, hunting, sporting heritage, diving and other outdoor activities.

HarperCollins Publishers NZ
P.O. Box 1, Auckland. Tel (09) 443 9400 Fax (09) 443 9403
Email editors@harpercollins.co.nz
Website www.harpercollins.co.nz
HarperCollins New Zealand is the local branch of the international HarperCollins publishing operation and is one of New Zealand's largest general publishers of non-fiction, fiction and children's books. Subject areas include natural history, sport, nautical, self-help, military, biography, history, Maori, current affairs and business. The company also has a general fiction list. Children's books are usually targeted at the 9–12 age group. The company prefers to accept manuscripts through agents or on the recommendation of a published author. Submissions should be made by post. Authors may expect a response within four to six weeks. Presentation guidelines are available on application.

Hazard Press
P.O. Box 2151, Christchurch.
Tel (03) 377 0370 Fax (03) 377 0390
Email info@hazard.co.nz
Website www.hazardpress.co.nz
Specialists in New Zealand poetry, biography and history.

Howling at the Moon Publishing and HATM Magazines
P.O. Box 302-188, North Harbour, North Shore 075.
Tel (09) 373 3676 Fax (09) 373 3667
Email ian@investigatemagazine.com
Website www.investigatemagazine.com
Investigative and current affairs books and magazines.

Huia Publishers
P.O. Box 17-335, Wellington.
Tel (04) 473 9262 Fax (04) 494 1838
Email comms@huia.co.nz
Huia publishes material in Maori or English (for both adults and children), including a growing commercial books list, educational resources and material that contributes to bicultural issues in Aotearoa. Material is acknowledged on receipt and decisions are generally reached within two months. Huia prefers being contacted by authors prior to them submitting manuscripts.

Hyndman Publishing
P.O. Box 19, Amberley. Tel (03) 314 9635 Fax (03) 314 9637
Email office@hyndman.co.nz
Website www.hyndman.co.nz
Publishers of cookbooks, gardening books, home and decorating books, diaries and journals.

Kotuku Media Ltd
P.O. Box 54-234, Plimmerton, Wellington. Tel (04) 233 1842
Specialises in New Zealand literature and authors. Its range of publications includes social history, biography, poetry, novels, politics, children's books (in English or Maori) and new age topics.

Kotuku Publishing
P.O. Box 22-011, Khandallah, Wellington
Tel (04) 479 3264 Fax (04) 479 8226
Fiction and non-fiction, especially for children. Material is not acknowledged on receipt. Decisions are usually reached within three weeks.

Learning Media Ltd
Private Bag 3293, Wellington. Tel (04) 472 5522 Fax (04) 472 6444
Email info@learningmedia.co.nz
Website www.learningmedia.co.nz
Learning Media is a state-owned publishing company that develops educational resources to support the curriculum from early childhood to tertiary levels. It also exports materials to North America, Europe, UK, Africa and the Pacific. Learning Media publishes resources in fourteen languages including English, Maori and six Pasifika languages.

David Ling Publishing Ltd
P.O. Box 34-601, Birkenhead, Auckland 0746. Tel & Fax (09) 418 2785
Email davidling@xtra.co.nz
Website www.davidling.co.nz
About 12 books a year are published by this company, including memoir, history, biography, general non-fiction and some fiction. David Ling Publishing is also active as a consultant and project co-ordinator, providing a complete editorial, design and manufacturing service for organisations, companies and individuals who wish to publish privately.

Longacre Press
P.O. Box 5340, Dunedin 9058. Tel (03) 477 2911 Fax (03) 477 7222
Email admin@longacre.co.nz
Website www.longacre.co.nz
Longacre Press is an independent publisher specialising in a broad range of New Zealand non-fiction, and junior and young adult fiction. The company publishes 18–20 titles per year. Imprints: Shoal Bay, Urban.

Macmillan Publishers New Zealand Ltd
Private Bag 102-970, North Shore Mail Centre, Auckland.
Tel (09) 414 0350 Fax (09) 414 0351
Email david@macmillan.co.nz
Website www.macmillan.co.nz
Macmillan develops and publishes texts for New Zealand secondary schools. Its interests include accounting, typing, economics, English, geography, history and social studies. Although it publishes only a small number of new titles each year, writers with appropriate educational backgrounds are invited to submit their ideas to the editor. Macmillan will also consider fiction for teenagers. Manuscripts are acknowledged, and decisions are reached within four to six weeks of receipt.

Mallinson Rendel Publishers Ltd
P.O. Box 9409, Wellington. Tel (04) 802 5012 Fax (04) 802 5013
Email ann@mallinsonrendel.co.nz

Mallinson Rendel specialises in children's picture books, junior and teenage fiction, publishing approximately seven new titles each year. The company will consider any manuscript for this age range; all submissions are acknowledged. Decisions can take anywhere between two weeks and three months. Guidelines are available, on request, about how material should be submitted.

The Mills Group Ltd
P.O. Box 30-818, Lower Hutt. Tel (04) 569 6744 Fax (04) 569 7464
The Mills Group publishes management books on sales, negotiation, motivation and related subjects.

National Pacific Press
PO Box 57-202 Mana, Porirua 5247. Tel & Fax (04) 233 8204
Email books@npp.co.nz
General publisher of 8–10 books a year in fiction, non-fiction and children's categories. NPP often works with first-time authors, helping them to become established in a very competitive marketplace. Unsolicited manuscripts are accepted but a preliminary enquiry is appreciated. Decisions on submitted manuscripts are usually made within 4–6 weeks.

New Holland Publishers (NZ) Ltd
P.O. Box 34-321, Birkenhead, Auckland.
Tel (09) 481 0444 Fax (09) 480 0129
Email help@nhp.co.nz
Website www.newhollandpublishers.co.nz
New Holland specialises in high-quality illustrated non-fiction titles with a particular focus on travel, lifestyle, natural history and hands-on guides to the outdoors. The company is also building a strong text-driven list in the areas of reference, personal finance and history. Proposals for new books within the specified areas are welcomed and are best posted, marked for the attention of the commissioning editor (see author information page for more detail on submissions). Every effort is made to respond to such proposals within four to six weeks.

New House Publishers
P.O. Box 33-376, Takapuna, Auckland 9.
Tel (09) 415 6853 Fax (09) 410 6850
Email service@newhouse.co.nz
Website www.newhouse.co.nz
New House Publishers specialise in high quality texts and workbooks for New Zealand secondary school students. All material should be relevant to the New Zealand curriculum. Also interested in specialist texts and juvenile fiction.

New Zealand Council for Educational Research
P.O. Box 3237, Wellington. Tel (04) 384 7939 Fax (04) 384 7933
Website www.nzcer.org.nz
NZCER is concerned solely with educational publishing, producing specialist reports on education, professional books for teachers, texts, educational histories and education periodicals.

New Zealand Playcentre Federation Publications
P.O. Box 15-886, New Lynn, Auckland.
Tel & Fax (09) 827 3469
Email publications@playcentre.org.nz
Website www.playcentre.org.nz
Publishes books of interest to early childhood educators, and parents of children at playcentres.

Nikau Press
P.O. Box 602, Nelson. Tel (03) 548 7537 Fax (03) 548 7535
Email nikau@ts.co.nz
Regional outdoor guides, natural history, local history and art books.

Otago Heritage Books
P.O. Box 6318, Dunedin. Tel & Fax (03) 477 1500
Email OtagoHeritageBooks@clear.net.nz
Southern regional history and reference.

Oxford University Press
P.O. Box 2784, Melbourne, Victoria, Australia. Tel 0800 442 502
OUP is now based in Melbourne but still publishes some New Zealand titles in the areas of economics, health science, law, Maori studies, history, politics, resource management, social science and women's studies, as well as reference books.

Pasifika Press
P.O. Box 68-446, Newton, Auckland.
Tel (09) 377 6068 Fax (09) 377 6069
Email press@pasifika.co.nz
Specialises in publications for and about the Pacific and its peoples.

Pearson Education
P.O. Box 102-902, North Shore Mail Centre, Auckland.
Tel (09) 442 7400 Fax (09) 442 7401
Email reception@pearsonnz.co.nz
Pearson Education has an extensive list of New Zealand educational titles in most areas of the curriculum for schools, polytechnics and universities. It does not publish general books such as fiction. Material is

acknowledged on receipt and decisions may be expected within one month. Pearson Education has detailed instructions for prospective authors and copies of these may be requested.

Penguin Group (NZ) Ltd
Private Bag 102-902, North Shore Mail Centre, Auckland 10.
Tel (09) 442 7400 Fax (09) 442 7401
Email books@penguin.co.nz
Website www.penguin.co.nz
As well as Penguin books, other imprints under the umbrella of this international publisher include Viking and Puffin. Both fiction and non-fiction appear in Penguin's New Zealand publishing programme. Fiction works include anthologies of verse and short stories, and novels; non-fiction titles fall into the following categories: archaeology, art, biography, business and politics, cookery, education, family, general, health, history, home and garden, Maori studies, natural history, New Zealand, the Pacific, lifestyle, sociology, sport and women. Penguin also publishes New Zealand children's fiction and non-fiction. For information on manuscript submissions, permissions and other information visit the 'About Us/Contact Information' page on the company's website. Note that manuscript submissions cannot be accepted by email.

Play*market*
P.O. Box 9767, Te Aro, Wellington.
Tel (04) 382 8462 Fax (04) 382 8461
Email info@playmarket.org.nz
Website www.playmarket.org.nz
A major distributor of published New Zealand plays, Play*market* is New Zealand's leading playwright agency, runs a script advisory/assessment service and holds workshops for promising new New Zealand plays (see Chapter 18 for full details).

Craig Potton Publishing
P.O. Box 555, Nelson. Tel (03) 548 9009 Fax (03) 548 9456
Email info@cpp.co.nz
New Zealand landscapes and pictorial books.

Profile Books
P.O. Box 5544, Wellesley Street, Auckland.
Tel (09) 630 8940 Fax (09) 630 1046
Website www.profile.co.nz
Books dealing with a broad range of business topics (a subsidiary of Profile Publishing).

Wendy Pye Ltd
Private Bag 17-905, Greenlane, Auckland.
Tel (09) 525 3575 Fax (09) 525 4205
Email info@sunshine.co.nz
Website www.sunshine.co.nz
Wendy Pye publishes a large number of children's fiction and non-fiction titles under the Sunshine Books imprint. The books published are mainly junior fiction readers, intended for use in classrooms, and feature a number of New Zealand authors. Series in science and other curriculum areas are also published.

Random House NZ
Private Bag 102-950, North Shore Mail Centre, Auckland 10.
Tel (09) 444 7197 Fax (09) 444 7524
Email admin@randomhouse.co.nz
Website www.randomhouse.co.nz
Random House NZ publishes New Zealand fiction, general non-fiction and children's fiction. Material received is acknowledged promptly and a decision on manuscripts can be expected after around two months.

Reed Publishing (NZ) Ltd
Private Bag 34-901, Birkenhead, Auckland 10.
Tel (09) 480 4950 Fax (09) 480 4999
Email info@reed.co.nz
Website www.reed.co.nz
Reed Publishing (NZ) Ltd, part of the Reed/Elsevier Group, publishes a wide range of titles each year. Areas of interest include: Maori, tramping, sport, history, fishing, fiction, guides, reference, natural history, pictorial, children's fiction and non-fiction. Prospective authors should refer to Reed's website for information on the over 350 New Zealand books in print.

RPL Books (Rugby Publishing Ltd)
P.O. Box 100-243, North Shore Mail Centre, Auckland.
Tel (09) 476 3510 Fax (09) 476 3590
Email rpl@rplbooks.co.nz
Sports biographies, general sports, computing and how-to titles.

Saint Publishing
P.O. Box 8157, Symonds St, Auckland.
Tel (09) 623 2510 or 0800 225 363 Fax (09) 623 2890
Email info@saintpublish.co.nz
Website www.saintpublish.co.nz

Specialist in retail and corporate calendars, and books on humour, sport and art.

Scholastic New Zealand Ltd
Private Bag 94-407, Greenmount, Auckland.
Tel (09) 274 8112 Fax (09) 274 8114
Email cdale@scholastic.co.nz
Website www.scholastic.co.nz
Scholastic New Zealand publishes a wide range of children's books which are distributed through the company's own book clubs and book fairs in schools, through retail outlets in New Zealand, and overseas through the international Scholastic group. Over 25 titles a year are published for young people aged from preschoolers to young adults. All material received is acknowledged, and final decisions on manuscripts can be expected within eight to twelve weeks.

SIR Publishing
P.O. Box 399, Wellington. Tel (04) 472 7421 Fax (04) 473 1841
Email sirp@rsnz.govt.nz.
Website www.rsnz.govt.nz
SIR Publishing is the publishing unit of The Royal Society of New Zealand. It was acquired from the former Department of Scientific and Industrial Research in July 1991. SIR Publishing publishes seven quarterly, national scientific journals of primary research and a range of educational and scientific leaflets, books and resource materials. The unit has six staff, which includes four scientific editors. Its research journals are distributed internationally via offices in New Zealand, the USA and the UK. Other scientific titles and educational resource materials are also available from its New Zealand office.

Te Reo Publications Ltd
P.O. Box 74, Opononi. Tel & Fax (09) 405 8116
Maori language books and resources, especially Ngapuhi dialect. Other publications planned of Northland writers, including in English.

Trans Pacific Marine
P.O. Box 1874, Auckland. Tel (09) 303 1459
Website www.transpacific.co.nz
Specialists in books about boat building, design, sailing and cruising.

Transpress New Zealand
12 Awanui Drive, Waikanae 5036; P.O. Box 10215, Wellington.
Tel (04) 293 3011 Fax (04) 293 3019
Email transpress@paradise.net.nz

Website www.transpressnz.homestead.com
Transpress (and its imprint IPL Books) publishes three to four trade titles a year and is interested in adult non-fiction which is of technical-historical, practical or reference interest. Writers should submit a synopsis of their manuscript in the first instance, along with details of illustrations that will accompany the work.

University of Otago Press
University of Otago, P.O. Box 56, Dunedin.
Tel (03) 479 8807 Fax (03) 474 8385
Email university.press@otago.ac.nz
The Press is committed to bringing readers the best of both worlds — special interest academic publications and general books for information and pure pleasure, with an Asia-Pacific focus. Titles range from Southern and Maori Studies through natural history to fiction.

Victoria University Press
P.O. Box 600, Wellington. Tel (04) 463 6580 Fax (04) 463 6581
Email victoria-press@vuw.ac.nz
Website www.vuw.ac.nz/vup
Victoria University Press is a major scholarly publisher specialising in New Zealand fiction, poetry, and plays; arts and literature; history; and New Zealand society.

Viking Sevenseas
P.O. Box 152, Paraparaumu. Tel/Fax 04 902 8240
Email vikings@paradise.net.nz
New Zealand natural history.

Waiatarua Publishing
P.O. Box 65-252, Mairangi Bay, Auckland. Tel (09) 415 3094
Children's fiction and non-fiction by New Zealand authors and artists.

Bridget Williams Books
P.O. Box 5482, Wellington. Tel (04) 473 8128
www.bwb.co.nz
New Zealand books in areas such as biography, contemporary issues, history, Maori subjects and women's studies.

Zealand Publishing House
Private Bag 12-029, Tauranga. Tel (07) 574 4114
Website www.zealandpublishing.co.nz
Health and self-improvement books. Also trades as Health House.

17 Awards, Competitions and Financial Assistance

Bank of New Zealand Katherine Mansfield Memorial Awards

The biennial Bank of New Zealand Katherine Mansfield Memorial Awards are New Zealand's pre-eminent short story awards. Commencing in 1959, the awards commemorate New Zealand's best-known writer and help New Zealand writers achieve recognition in their own country. They are this country's longest-running creative writing awards.

In 2006 there were three award categories. The Bank of New Zealand Katherine Mansfield Award is open to unpublished stories, and offers a first prize of $10,000 and a second prize of $1,500 for stories up to 5,000 words. The Bank of New Zealand Novice Writers Award is open to writers who have never been published, and offers a first prize of $1,500 for stories up to 3,000 words. The Bank of New Zealand Young Writers Award is open to unpublished stories by secondary school authors, and offers a first prize of $1,000 (plus $500 to the winner's school) for stories up to 2,500 words.

Ursula Bethell Residency in Creative Writing

Created to foster New Zealand writing, this position provides an opportunity for a writer to work full-time in an academic environment. The position is open to writers of fiction, poetry or drama, and the appointment is made on the basis of published or performed writing of high quality. The $46,500 emolument is jointly funded by the University of Canterbury and Creative New Zealand, and is granted for up to one year. The closing date for applications is usually the end of September. Information and an application form are available from The Registrar, University of Canterbury, Private Bag 4800, Christchurch.

Buddle Findlay Sargeson Fellowship

In 1997 Buddle Findlay joined forces with The Sargeson Trust and became the inaugural commercial sponsor of the Buddle Findlay Sargeson Fellowship. The fellowship is unique in New Zealand as it is the country's only residential writing fellowship. Applicants must be published writers of poetry or fiction. Selected New Zealand writers are provided with a furnished studio flat in The Sargeson Centre in central Auckland and a stipend of $20,000.The fellowship may be shared by up to two fellows and tenure is from March through to December. Applications close early in November each year. Further information and application forms are available from the Marketing Dept, Buddle Findlay, P.O. Box 1433, Auckland, or visit www.buddlefindlay.co.nz

Burns Fellowship (Otago University)
Open to writers of imaginative literature — including drama, fiction, poetry and biography - who are resident in New Zealand. The fellowship is worth $46,000. Fellows must live and work in Dunedin during the time of the fellowship. The closing date for applications is early August and details and application forms may be requested from Human Resources, University of Otago, P.O. Box 56, Dunedin.

Russell Clark Award
The award will be made to the illustrator or artist for the most distinguished pictures or illustrations for a children's book, with or without text. The artist or illustrator must be a citizen or resident of New Zealand. The award is in the form of a medal and a sum of money from the Library and Information Association of New Zealand Aotearoa (LIANZA). The award is usually announced at the annual conference at the Children's Book Awards ceremony, with publishers being invited to provide entries each year for this annual award. Further details may be obtained from LIANZA, P.O. Box 12-212, Wellington. Email office@lianza.org.nz.

Creative New Zealand
Creative New Zealand is the main arts development organisation in New Zealand and the only national organisation able to allocate funding to projects that span all the art forms. Financial support for writers' and publishers' projects and for literary organisers is available. Applicants can choose which funding programme to apply under but they must meet specific eligibility conditions.

All applicants for writing grants must be published writers, but need not have published a book. A reasonable track record would be several pieces of work published in anthologies or established literary journals. It is an advantage to have a publishing history in the genre for which you are seeking funding.

Publishers should also have a track record with good access to marketing, promotion and distribution networks. Literary event organisers must be able to demonstrate their ability to promote New Zealand literature and to provide full financial details of the projects for which they seek support. Creative New Zealand supports specific items, e.g. speaking fees for writers at festivals or specific touring costs, rather than a predicted 'shortfall' in an overall budget.

The *Todd New Writers' Bursary* and the *Louis Johnson New Writers' Bursary* are awarded by the Arts Board each year to emerging writers who have a small but promising track record. The Todd Foundation contributes a half-share of the $20,000 per annum Todd New Writers' Bursary, which allows a promising new writer to work full-time on an approved project. Interest from a monetary gift, made in 1989 by poet Louis Johnson's estate, contributes to the $18,000 Louis Johnson New Writers' Bursary which has a duration of six months.

You cannot apply for the new writers' bursaries. The two bursaries are awarded each year to writers who are identified as being at an early stage in their writing career and who apply for a writing grant to the July deadline. If you wish, you can signal in your covering letter or project outline that you hope to be considered for one of the bursaries.

The *Creative New Zealand Writer's Residency in Berlin* was set up by the Arts Board to provide a unique opportunity for an established writer of New Zealand literature who has been resident in New Zealand for at least three years and who has published one or more books. Priority is given to works of fiction, poetry, drama, biography or history which is of national significance to New Zealand arts topics. It provides return travel to Germany, a rent-free flat in Berlin, and a stipend of $3,000 per month for ten months. Currently, it runs from September to June. Further information is available on request from the Arts Adviser, Literature. The primary aim will be for the writer to work on an approved project while in Berlin, with priority given to fiction, poetry, drama, biography, New Zealand history, or New Zealand arts. On returning from Berlin, the writer will be expected to have completed, or substantially completed, a body of writing, and should be able to demonstrate other tangible benefits to New Zealand literature. Application should be by letter, accompanied by a literary CV, a detailed project proposal and up to ten pages of work in progress.

The *International Writing Program, University of Iowa, USA* — in partnership with the University of Iowa International Writing Program, the Arts Board of Creative New Zealand offers a three-month residency for a New Zealand writer. The residency is suitable for nationally recognised writers of fiction, poetry, drama, children's fiction, screenplays, biography or cultural commentary, who have previously published at least one volume of work.

For full information and a copy of the funding guide, contact Creative New Zealand, P.O. Box 3806, Wellington. Tel (04) 473 0880 Fax (04) 471 2865. Email info@creativenz.govt.nz Website www.creativenz.govt.nz

Tom Fitzgibbon Award

This award is administered by the Children's Literature Foundation of New Zealand and sponsored by Scholastic New Zealand. It was named to recognise the outstanding contribution made by the late Tom Fitzgibbon to the growth and status of children's literature in New Zealand. The award is made annually when merited, to a previously unpublished author. It carries a monetary prize of $1,500 and an offer of publication by Scholastic

New Zealand. The manuscript must be a work of fiction of at least 10,000 words, and be appropriate for children aged 7–13 years. Entries close on 31 October each year. Brochures with detailed information and entry forms are available from the Convenor, Tom Fitzgibbon Award, Children's Literature Foundation of New Zealand Inc., P.O. Box 96-094, Balmoral, Auckland. There is a $10 entry fee. Visit www.storylines.org.nz for more information.

Esther Glen Award
The award will be made to the author of the book that is considered to be the most distinguished contribution to literature for children, by an author who is a citizen or resident of New Zealand. The award is in the form of a medal and a sum of money from the Library and Information Association of New Zealand Aotearoa (LIANZA). The award is usually announced at the annual conference at the Children's Book Awards ceremony, with publishers being invited to provide entries each year for this annual award. Further details may be obtained from LIANZA, P.O. Box 12-212, Wellington.
Email office@lianza.org.nz.

Foxton Fellowship
For writers of fiction, drama or poetry who are NZ Society of Authors members, this fellowship offers $5,000 and a one-month residency at a cottage at Foxton Beach on the Horowhenua coast. Applicants should send a C.V. with their application. They should either have published a book already, or have a substantial amount published in literary journals, or (in the case of dramatists) produced for stage or screen. The residency may be taken up during any month mutually agreed by the fellow and the owners of the cottage. Closing date for applications is 30 September. For details contact the New Zealand Society of Authors, P.O. Box 67-013, Mt Eden, Auckland 3, or email nzsa@clear.net.nz.

John Harris Award
The John Harris Award is presented by the Library and Information Association of New Zealand Aotearoa (LIANZA) in recognition of notable published work, such as in the bibliographical, critical, historical or administrative fields, which represents a contribution to New Zealand librarianship. The award consists of a sum of money and an appropriate diploma and is only awarded when merited. Nominations should be submitted by July 1. Details may be obtained from LIANZA, P.O. Box 12-212, Wellington. Email admin@lianza.org.nz.

Louis Johnson New Writers' Bursary
(See Creative New Zealand entry earlier in this chapter.)

Te Kura Pounamu Award
The Library and Information Association of New Zealand Aotearoa (LIANZA) offers annually an award, known as the Te Kura Pounamu Award to a writer

selected from nominees submitted by publishers by April 1. The award will be made to the author of a book that is considered to be a distinguished contribution to literature for children or young people, written in Te Reo Maori. The author shall be a citizen or resident of Aotearoa New Zealand. The award is in the form of a greenstone pendant and $1000 from LIANZA. The award is usually announced at the annual conference at the Children's Book Awards ceremony, with publishers being invited to provide entries each year for this annual award. Further details may be obtained from LIANZA, P.O. Box 12-212, Wellington. Email admin@lianza.org.nz.

The Elsie Locke Award
The Library and Information Association of New Zealand Aotearoa offers annually an award known as the LIANZA Young People's Non-Fiction Award. The award shall be made for a work that is considered to be a distinguished contribution to non-fiction for young people. The recipient of the award shall be a citizen or resident of New Zealand. The award is in the form of a medal and $1000 from the Library and Information Association of New Zealand Aotearoa (LIANZA). Further details may be obtained from LIANZA, P.O. Box 12-212, Wellington. Email admin@lianza.org.nz.

Media Peace Awards
This annual award recognises media professionals and students who actively contribute towards reducing conflict, addressing differences and counteracting prejudice in society. Details can be obtained from the Peace Foundation, P.O. Box 4110, Auckland. Tel (09) 373 2379
Email peace@fps.pl.net Website www.peace.net.nz.

Bank of NZ Katherine Mansfield Memorial Fellowship
This award is sponsored by the Bank of New Zealand and managed by Creative New Zealand on behalf of the Katherine Mansfield Memorial Trust. This fellowship is offered annually to enable a New Zealand writer to work in Menton, France, for a period of not less than four months during the year of tenure. Applicants must be New Zealanders by birth or by registration, or have been resident in New Zealand continuously for a period of ten years prior to making an application. Applicants must be dedicated writers who would use the Fellowship to further their literary studies and endeavour. When considering applications, the selection committee will take into account the sources of assistance applicants may have for full-time writing and travel. The Katherine Mansfield memorial room at the Villa Isola Bella, Menton, has been furnished as a study and the Fellow should be prepared to make the fullest possible use of this room as headquarters for writing and/or studying during the tenure period. Accommodation is not provided by the Fellowship. The amount available to the Fellow will not be less than NZ$55,000, from which the Fellow should allow for travel costs and insurance. Applications close in July each year. More information about

terms and conditions is available from Creative New Zealand, P.O. Box 3806, Wellington. Tel (04) 473 0880 Fax (04) 471 2865
Email info@creativenz.govt.nz Website www.creativenz.govt.nz.

Montana New Zealand Book Awards
The Montana New Zealand Book Awards, sponsored by Montana Wines and supported by Creative New Zealand, recognise excellence in New Zealand writing. Three awards are presented for new writing: The New Zealand Society of Authors Hubert Church Best First Book of Fiction Award, The New Zealand Society of Authors Jessie MacKay Best First Book of Poetry Award, and The New Zealand Society of Authors E. H. McCormick Best First Book Award for Non-Fiction. Five non-fiction category awards were presented: Lifestyle and Contemporary Culture, Poetry, Environment, History and Biography, Reference and Anthology and Illustrative Arts. From these categories a winner was chosen for the Montana Medal, being the book considered the best from any non-fiction category. The best book of fiction in any year is awarded the Deutz Medal for Fiction. Also awarded is the Reader's Choice Award, being the shortlisted title selected through a nationwide voting process as the most popular with the reading public. The NZ Society of Authors' best First Book Award and the A.W. Reed Award for contribution to NZ literature are awarded at the ceremony. Submissions for entries are called in late October of each year and cover the period 1 April of that year to 31 March of the year in which the awards are made. Further details are available from Booksellers New Zealand, P.O. Box 13-248, Johnsonville, Wellington. Tel (04) 478 5511 Fax (04) 478 5519, visit the website www.booksellers.co.nz or email info@booksellers.co.nz

National Library Research Fellowship
In order to encourage the scholarly use of its collections, especially those in the Alexander Turnbull Library, and the production of works based upon them, the National Library of New Zealand offers a fellowship to the value of $45,000 per annum. Applications close at the end of September. Further details, guidelines and application forms may be requested from the Secretary, National Library Research Fellowship Committee, P.O. Box 12-349, Wellington or email atl@nat.lib.govt.nz

New Zealand Authors' Fund
The New Zealand Authors' Fund compensates New Zealand authors for the loss of income through holdings of their books in New Zealand libraries. Authors may register with the fund if they are eligible to receive royalties for their books and if more than 50 copies are held in New Zealand libraries. Creative New Zealand's guidelines explain in detail who can register, how to determine if your book qualifies, how to register, and so on. Further information about the fund and registration details may be obtained from Creative New Zealand, P.O. Box 3806, Wellington. Tel (04) 473 0880

Fax (04) 471 2865 Email authors.fund@creativenz.govt.nz
Website www.creativenz.govt.nz.

New Zealand History Research Trust Fund
The New Zealand History Research Trust Fund offers financial support for the researching and writing of all areas of New Zealand history (non-fiction), with preference given to projects that would significantly improve the understanding of New Zealand's past. Awards may be made to individuals or groups and reimburse research, travel, equipment and living costs. Assistance is not normally available for projects that are eligible for tertiary research funds, nor for tertiary theses. An average of eighty applications are received each year and $88,000–$90,000 is disbursed annually among the ten to twelve applicants who receive awards. Applications close on 15 October each year. Further information and application forms can be obtained from New Zealand History Research Trust Fund, History Group, Ministry for Culture and Heritage, P.O. Box 5364, Wellington. Tel (04) 496 6355 Fax (04) 499 4490. Email historyaward@mch.govt.nz Website www.mch.govt.nz/awards/history.

New Zealand Post Book Awards for Children and Young Adults
Sponsored by New Zealand Post, supported by Creative New Zealand, and managed by Booksellers New Zealand and Book Tokens NZ Ltd, these awards provide recognition for authors and illustrators of high-quality New Zealand literature for children. Seven awards are presented: New Zealand Post Book of the Year (drawn from the four category winners), Young Adult Award, Junior Fiction Award, Non-Fiction Award, Picture Book Award, Best First Book Award and The Children's Choice Award. Submissions are called in September and close in December for books published in the twelve-month period January to December of that year. Further details are available from Booksellers New Zealand, P.O. Box 13-248, Johnsonville, Wellington. Tel (04) 478 5511. Email info@booksellers.co.nz
Website www.nzpostbookawards.co.nz.

NZSA Mentoring Programme
Selected writers who can demonstrate potential and commitment are offered an opportunity to work closely with a mentor for 20 hours over a period of up to 12 months. Mentors make themselves available to discuss ideas and problems, provide editorial advice, and share the benefit of their experience as published writers. Mentoring may be may be phone, fax, email, post or face to face. The scheme is available to NZ Society of Authors members only, subject to available funding, who have a substantial work in progress. Closing date for applications is 31 March. For details contact the New Zealand Society of Authors, P.O. Box 67-013, Mt Eden, Auckland 1349, or email nzsa@clear.net.nz.

New Zealand Young Playwrights Competition
An annual competition for 16 to 22-year-old NZ residents who are asked to submit a one-act play (more than 30 minutes in length) in English or Te Reo Maori. Six winners are chosen spread across three geographical regions. The winners receive a cash prize of $250 and a workshop of their play with a professional director and dramaturge (literary advisor for theatre and film). Applications should be typed and include the playwright's name and contact details. The deadline for applications in any given year can be obtained by contacting Play*market*, P.O. Box 9767, Te Aro, Wellington. Tel (04) 382 8462. Email scripts@playmarket.org.nz. A panel of judges makes the decision, which is then final. No correspondence can be entered into.

J. M. Sherrard Awards
Biennial awards totalling $1,000, for studies in New Zealand local and regional history, are offered by the Canterbury Historical Association. Enquiries should be made to the Canterbury Historical Association, c/o Department of History, University of Canterbury, Private Bag 4800, Christchurch. No entry is required — the judges assess all likely titles appearing in the national bibliography.

NZSA Lilian Ida Smith Award
A prize of $3,000 is awarded to assist in the completion of a fiction, non-fiction, poetry or drama project. This biennial award is open to NZSA members over the age of 35 and closes on 1 March. Details may be requested from The Secretary, New Zealand Society of Authors, P.O. Box 67-013, Mt Eden, Auckland 1349.

Bruce Mason Playwriting Award
An annual award of $7,000 originally presented by INL in memory of their most famous reporter, is administered by Play*market*. This award is presented in order to recognise early success in the career of the winning playwright and to encourage their continued exploration of the theatre medium. The award is supported by the Arts Foundation of NZ and Downstage Theatre Society. Applications are submitted by major theatre companies and awards include a full-length play commission and annual play reading.

Todd New Writers' Bursary
(See Creative New Zealand entry earlier in this chapter.)

Auckland University Literary Fellowship
The Fellowship has been created jointly by the University of Auckland and Creative New Zealand to foster New Zealand writing by providing a full-time opportunity to work in an academic environment. The position, which is available annually for a period of one year, is open to anyone in the field of creative writing. Applicants should be writers of proven merit and be normally resident in New Zealand. The Fellow will be required to reside in

Auckland for the term of the appointment. A stipend of up to $50,300 per annum (subject to taxation) will be paid. Appointment is confirmed subject to Creative New Zealand funding. Conditions of appointment and method of application are available from the Academic Appointments Section, Auckland University, Private Bag 92-019, Auckland.

University of Waikato Writer-in-Residence
This award enables a New Zealand writer of fiction, poetry, drama, non-fiction or children's literature, writing in English or Maori, to become the University's Writer-in-Residence. The award was created to foster New Zealand writing by providing a full-time opportunity for a writer to work in an academic environment. It is sponsored jointly by the University of Waikato and Creative New Zealand, and is administered by the University of Waikato. Applicants should be authors of proven merit, normally resident in New Zealand, or New Zealanders temporarily resident overseas. The Writer will be required to reside in Hamilton for the period of the appointment. It is expected that a Writer will take up the appointment in February each year for a period of 12 months. The taxable income for this award is $36,000. Applications close at the end of September. Enquiries may be made to the Director, Human Resource Management Division, The University of Waikato, Private Bag 3105, Hamilton.

Victoria University Writer-in-Residence
This fellowship is open to writers in all areas of literary activity, including drama, fiction, poetry, New Zealand art, geography, music, biography and history. Applicants should be New Zealand authors of proven merit. The fellowship, funded jointly by Victoria University and the New Zealand Literary Fund, is for a nine-month academic year and requires no formal teaching. Applications normally close in early September, and details and application forms may be requested from The Human Resources Assistant, Faculty of Humanities and Social Sciences, Victoria University, P.O. Box 600, Wellington. Email hss-appoint@vuw.ac.nz

F. P. Wilson Book Award
A biennial award of $500 is made to the author of a New Zealand history work judged to be the most distinguished contribution to New Zealand history over the past two years. Details may be requested from the Department of History, Victoria University, P.O. Box 600, Wellington.
Email history@vuw.ac.nz

Robert Lord Writer's Trust
Writers in any genre eligible to apply for tenure of a rent-free Dunedin cottage (bequeathed by Robert Lord), from three months to two years, to undertake writing projects. May be held in conjunction with other grants or awards. For more information contact the Writer's Trust c/- Playmarket, P.O. Box 9767, Wellington. Email info@playmarket.org.nz

Pacific Writer's Residency
Fullbright–Creative NZ residency at the University of Hawaii open to New Zealand-based writers of Pacific Island heritage who have had work published previously, are New Zealand citizens and are working on a specific project. Tenure from late August to late November. Grant includes return airfares to Hawaii, rental accommodation for three months, and a $NZ6,000 stipend. For further information contact Anton Carter, Arts Advisor, Pacific Arts, Creative NZ, P.O. Box 3806, Wellington.

International Writing Programme, University of Iowa
Open to recognised writers of fiction, poetry, drama, children's fiction, screenplays, biography or cultural commentary who have had at least one previous work published. Programme fosters New Zealand writers working on a major project while participating with other international writers. Three-month tenure includes stipend to cover travel and per diem food and accommodation on campus. In partnership with Creative NZ. For more information apply to Arts Advisor, Creative Literature, Creative NZ, P.O. Box 3806, Wellington.

There are many small competitions and awards. The NZ Book Council has a list of other awards on their website's competition noticeboard. Visit www.bookcouncil.org.nz

18 Organisations

New Zealand Society of Authors

(formerly PEN New Zealand Inc.)

Founded more than 60 years ago as the PEN New Zealand Centre, NZSA is the local arm of a worldwide organisation working for writers. NZSA provides a voice for New Zealand writers on legal and moral issues, makes representations on their behalf to the Government and other organisations, monitors copyright and censorship, and works with New Zealand publishers to protect the rights of authors in this country.

Services

NZSA has drawn up an annotated model standard contract to help inexperienced authors — it is intended for use directly with publishers, or as a basis for comparison with any book contract writers may be offered. *The Business of Writing* is available to members at a minimal charge. Non-members should enquire for current charges.

A Legal Advice Committee exists to help members with any problems, in particular with matters concerning copyright and contracts. In some cases, NZSA members may be offered subsidised legal help. Members should, in the first instance, contact the executive director.

A bimonthly journal, *The New Zealand Author*, is published to keep members informed about NZSA's activities — it contains a wealth of regular, up-to-date information about publishing opportunities and writing developments in New Zealand and overseas.

The society has six branches around the country which provide a forum for discussions on matters of interest to writers. It runs several awards and fellowships in addition to a mentoring programme (see Chapter 17 for details).

NZSA works closely with Creative New Zealand, the Book Council and copyright organisations.

Management and membership

NZSA's administrative business is conducted by an executive director and a part-time secretary under the direction of the National Council, with the authority of the annual general meeting. Between meetings, the centre is serviced by the president and vice-presidents.

Ordinary membership is offered to those with a suitable list of writing credits. Associate membership is offered to people with a serious interest in writing and writers. Associate members may convert to ordinary membership at any time by submitting a list of suitable writing credits to the executive. Both kinds of members are very welcome.

Application forms and further details about the New Zealand Society of Authors, its membership benefits, fees and activities, may be requested from NZSA, P.O. Box 67-013, Mt Eden, Auckland 3. Tel & Fax (09) 379 4801 Email office@nzauthors.org.nz

Play*market*

Since 1973 this non-profit incorporated society has worked to develop and promote work by New Zealand playwrights. Currently funded by Creative New Zealand, Play*market* offers a range of services focused on writing scripts for the stage.

Any New Zealand playwright can send a script to Play*market* for an assessment of its strengths, weaknesses and production potential. Scripts must be typed on one side of the page only and must be accompanied by a synopsis, cast list, self-addressed envelope and a cheque for $100. The playwright then receives an assessment prepared by an experienced professional theatre practitioner within three weeks of the submission of the script. Play*market* also offers a further assessment service in which the writer is provided with a written report and an hour-long script consultation. The fee for this service is $150. The same requirements for the submission of scripts apply.

Play*market* also organises readings and workshops for selected scripts. These script development services are offered at the discretion of Play*market*. Application forms for script development assistance, which outline the criteria for being considered a suitable applicant for such assistance, can be obtained from Play*market*.

Play*market* is the country's principal playwrights' agency, circulating and promoting scripts to producers, negotiating contracts, and collecting and distributing royalties. Around 175 productions are licensed annually for shows that generate more than $2.5 million at the box office. Play*market* invites specific playwrights to appoint them as agent and is primarily focused on stage productions in New Zealand and Australia. There are currently approximately 150 client writers and associates on its books, including New Zealand's most successful and best-loved playwrights.

Play*market* publishes a quarterly magazine, Play*market* News, and operates a tiered membership scheme which allows access to news of playwriting competitions and other information of interest to writers ($30 for Fans, $50 for Groupies and $95 for Angels). Play*market* operates a mail-order system from its website for the purchase of published and unpublished New Zealand scripts. Play*market* also contributes funds to the annual Adam Play Reading series. The Adam Play Reading series showcases New Zealand plays which are in development or have not previously been seen by a Wellington audience.

Further information is available from Play*market*, P.O. Box 9767, Te Aro, Wellington. Tel (04) 382 8462 Fax (04) 382 8461

Email info@playmarket.org.nz Website www.playmarket.org.nz.

Manuscript assessors

The NZ Association of Manuscript Assessors is a group of professional editors and writers who offer authors objective advice and guidance on how to bring their work closer to publishable standard. All members have worked in manuscript assessing, editing and/or the teaching of writing. NZAMA has a strict code of professional practice and entry criteria.

Fleur Beale — Fiction for children and young adults (not picture books or poetry).
Email fleurbeale@clear.net.nz Tel (04) 387 2255

Norman Bilbrough — Work for children, fiction and non-fiction.
Email norman.b@paradise.net.nz Tel (04) 476 5316

Jill Marshall — General fiction, work for children.
Email jillmarshall@ihug.co.nz

Lesley Marshall — Fiction, including romance, non-fiction including theses, family history.
Email editline@xtra.co.nz Tel (09) 434 6814

Barbara Murison — children's books, young adult and picture books.
Email barbaram@clear.net.nz Tel (04) 479 5538

Jane Parkin — fiction (not children or young adults)
Email jane@paradise.net.nz Tel (04) 388 4535

Pen and Ink Services, Loren Teague — Fiction, including romance, crime, fantasy, historical, thriller, young adult and other genres.
Email pen-ink@netaccess.co.nz. Tel 03 547 5369

Poygraphia, Dr Calum Gilmour — Non-fiction and academic texts.
Email info@polygraphianz.com Tel (09) 416 1437

Anna Rogers — Fiction and non-fiction (no work for children or young adults).
Email a.rogers@paradise.net.nz Tel (03) 379 6558

Total Fiction Services — Fiction, non-fiction, children's and young adult fiction, poetry.
Barbara Else Email barbara@elseware.co.nz
Chris Else Email chris@elseware.co.nz
Emma Neale Email ejneale@ihug.co.nz

Write Right — Novels, autobiographies, travel books, short stories, children's and technical.
Graeme Lay Email graemelay@xtra.co.nz
Tina Shaw Email programmes@nzauthors.org.nz
Stephen Stratford Email stephen.stratford@xtra.co.nz

Literary agents and publishing consultants

It is important to understand what is offered by these services, some of which will assess, edit and prepare your work for submission and act as agents, while others offer to sell your script to a publisher. If you are a new author the former will probably help you most.

Always send a SAE and ask for full information as to exactly what an agency will do, their fees, and a list of their published authors, before agreeing to go ahead with any of the services. (See more about agents in Chapter One.)

Glenys Bean Literary Agency
P.O. Box 6050, Titirangi, Auckland.
Tel (09) 812 8486 Fax (09) 812 8188
Email g.bean@clear.net.nz
Website www.glenysbean.com

Book Lovers International
P.O. Box 331-677, Takapuna, Auckland.
Tel (09) 486 6328 Fax (09) 486 6398

Bookprint Consultants Ltd
6/9 Wilkinson Street, Oriental Bay, Wellington.
Tel (04) 381 3071 Fax (04) 381 3067
Email gstewart@iconz.co.nz

Dunsford Publishing Consultants-Global Dialogues
RD6, Warkworth.
Website www.dunsfordpublishing.com
Email dunsford.publishing@xtra.co.nz

Fraser Books
Ranginui, Chamberlain Road, RD 8, Masterton.
Tel (06) 377 1359
Email ifgrant@xtra.co.nz

Michael Gifkins and Assoicates
P.O. Box 6496, Auckland. Tel (09) 523 5032 Fax (09) 523 5033
Mob 021 522 278
Email michael.gifkins@xtra.co.nz

Richards Literary Agency
P.O. Box 31-240, Milford, Auckland. Tel/Fax (09) 410 0209
Email rla.richards@clear.net.nz

Total Fiction Services (TFS)
P.O. Box 46-031, Lower Hutt, Wellington. Tel & Fax (04) 565 4429
Email tfs@elseware.co.nz
Website www.elseware.co.nz

Write Right
P.O. Box 56-112, Dominion Road, Auckland.
Tel (09) 623 7331 Fax (09) 623 7353
Email stephen.stratford@xtra.co.nz

Other organisations

There are many organisations of interest to New Zealand writers, varying from national publishing bodies and statutory organisations to small, informal societies catering for specialist interests. All of the organisations listed below have some connection with publishing in New Zealand. For further information on their activities and services, you should contact them directly.

Book Publishers' Association of New Zealand Inc
P.O. Box 36-477, Northcote, Auckland.
Tel (09) 480 2711 Fax (09) 480 1130
Email bpanz@copyright.co.nz

Booksellers New Zealand
P.O. Box 13-248, Johnsonville, Wellington.
Tel (04) 478 5511 Fax (04) 478 5519
Email info@booksellers.co.nz

Copyright Council of New Zealand Inc
P.O. Box 5028, Wellington. Tel (04) 472 4430
Website www.copyright.org.nz

Copyright Licensing Ltd
P.O. Box 36-477, Northcote, Auckland.
Tel (09) 480 2711 Fax (09) 480 1130
Email cll@copyright.co.nz

Copyright Publications Office
General Assembly Library, Parliament Buildings, Wellington.

Creative New Zealand
National office: P.O. Box 3806, Wellington.
Tel (04) 473 0880 Fax (04) 471 2865
Email info@creativenz.govt.nz
Northern office: P.O. Box 1425, Auckland.
Tel (09) 373 3066 Fax (09) 377 6795
Email northern@creativenz.govt.nz
Southern office: P.O. Box 2932, Christchurch.
Tel (03) 366 2337 Fax (03) 366 9199
Email southern@creativenz.govt.nz

ISBN & ISSN Agencies
ISBN Librarian
National Library of New Zealand, P.O. Box 1467, Wellington.
Tel (04) 474 3074 Fax (04) 474 3161
Email isbn@natlib.govt.nz .
ISSN Librarian
National Library of New Zealand, P.O. Box 1467, Wellington.
Tel (04) 474 3090 Fax (04) 474 3161
Email issn@natlib.govt.nz

Legal Deposit Office
P.O. Box 12-340, 58-78 Molesworth Street, Wellington.
Tel (04) 474 3104 Fax (04) 474 3161
Email legal.deposit@natlib.govt.nz

LIANZA (Library and Information Association of New Zealand Aotearoa)
P.O. Box 12-212, Thorndon, Wellington.
Tel (04) 473 5834 Fax (04) 499 1480
Email office@lianza.org.nz
Website www.lianza.org.nz

National Library Society
P.O. Box 12-514, Wellington. Tel (04) 389 7103 Fax (04) 389 7301
Email peterthorp@xtra.co.nz
Website www.natlib.govt.nz

New Zealand Book Council
Level 7, Navigate House, 69 Boulcott St, Wellington.
Tel (04) 499 1569 Fax (04) 499 1424
Email admin@bookcouncil.org.nz
Website www.bookcouncil.org.nz

Nielsen BookData
PO Box 46-018, Herne Bay, Auckland.
Tel (09) 360 3294 Fax (09) 360 8853
Email data@nielsenbookdata.co.nz
Website: www.nielsenbookdata.co.nz

Storylines: Children's Literature Foundation of New Zealand Inc
P.O. Box 96-094, Balmoral, Auckland. Tel/Fax (09) 630 0514
Email childlitnz@storylines.org.nz
Website: www.storylines.org.nz

New Zealand Poetry Society
P.O. Box 5283, Lambton Quay, Wellington.
Email info@poetrysociety.org.nz
Website www.poetrysociety.org.nz

New Zealand Press Council
P.O. Box 10-879, The Terrace, Wellington.
Tel (04) 473 5220 Fax (04) 471 1785
Email presscouncil@asa.co.nz
Website: www.presscouncil.org.nz

New Zealand Writers Guild
P.O. Box 47-886, Ponsonby, Auckland.
Tel (09) 360 1408 Fax (09) 360 1409
Email info@nzwritersguild.co.nz
Website www.nzwritersguild.org.nz

19 Courses for New Zealand

This section is intended to be a brief summary of journalism and writing courses offered in New Zealand — but, naturally enough, details of courses and their content may change from time to time. If you are considering enrolling for any of the programmes outlined below, you are advised to contact the registrar or principal of the institution concerned for up-to-date information.

Aoraki Polytechnic
Private Bag 902, Timaru.
Tel (03) 684 8240 Freephone 0800 4 AORAKI Fax (03) 684 0809
Email study@aoraki.ac.nz
Website www.aoraki.ac.nz
Range of courses at varying levels covering creative writing, print journalism, radio and television journalism and production and general media studies. Different courses are available at campuses in Timaru, Dunedin and Christchurch. These include:
National Diploma in Journalism (Print) and Media Communication — an intensive 34-week full-time programme with a strong practical focus, including news writing, news gathering, media law, reporting on court, police, local government and Treaty of Waitangi issues, shorthand for journalism, interviewing skills, feature writing and research.
National Diploma in Journalism (Television and Radio) — an intensive one-year full-time programme where students learn core journalism skills and gain specialised training in either radio or television news reporting, including four weeks' practical experience at a television or radio newsroom. The National Certificate in Journalism is a stepping stone to this course.
Advanced Certificate in Creative Writing — a 34-week part-time programme catering for those who are serious about writing and already competent in language skills, which aims to develop writing skills that can be applied to a wide range of genres including poetry and non-

fiction. The writing process, structural options, narrative technique, etc, are explored as well as specific genres such as children's, poetry, biography and memoir.

Introduction to Freelance Writing — this 20-week part-time programme enables students to gain an understanding of the basic approaches to successful freelance writing. Students will learn various writing styles, structures and presentations.

Certificate in Media Communication — the aim of this 34-week full-time study programme is to provide students with foundation skills in broadcast and print journalism, studio operation and fundamentals of feature story writing, filming and recording.

Auckland University of Technology
Private Bag 92-006, Auckland.
Tel (09) 921 9999 Fax (09) 921 9985 Freephone 0800 aut uni
Email courseinfo@aut.ac.nz
Website www.aut.ac.nz

Graduate Diploma in Journalism — a one-year intensive full-time programme for students who have completed a tertiary qualification and wish to enter the media industry, and for people with relevant work experience wanting to increase their skills. Subjects include interviewing and information gathering, news writing, shorthand, media theory, and editing and design; options include magazine writing, radio and television journalism, and writing for the new technology and online publications.

Bachelor of Communication Studies — a three-year full-time degree that offers theoretical and practical experience over a wide range of communication fields. Option in year three to specialise in one area, such as broadcast or media journalism and the creative industries. Core modules include newspaper editing and design, the different writing specialisations, bicultural reporting, media law and ethics. Public affairs reporting examines court and government work (both local and national), and students learn how to take notes in shorthand.

AUT also offers a range of certificate and diploma courses and the following short courses:

Writing (Advanced Professional) — eight weeks, 16 hours, part-time; a step-by-step transition through the stages of the writing process, including the keys to successful writing in the workplace, collecting and summarising relevant information, planning, writing drafts, editing for sense and proof-reading for accuracy, and presentation.

Writing (News Media) — ten weeks, 30 hours, part-time; an in-depth look at writing styles and how they are tailored to a target audience.

Writing (Practical) — a six-week (12 hours) course that aims to improve your accuracy in writing and understanding of the basic techniques of writing for specific purposes, including spelling, punctuation and grammar, construction of sentences and paragraphs, and writing and reviewing effective memos, letters and reports.

Christchurch Polytechnic Institute of Technology
New Zealand Broadcasting School, P.O. Box 540, Christchurch.
Tel (03) 940 8072, 0800 242476
Email info@cpit.ac.nz
Website www.cpit.ac.nz
Bachelor of Broadcasting Communications (Broadcast Journalism) — a degree programme held over 2½ years that specialises in applied journalism skills, with particular emphasis on radio and television journalism.

Also offers part-time 20 week (32 hours) courses in communications.

Manukau Institute of Technology
Private Bag 94-006, Manukau City, Auckland.
Tel 0800 626252 Fax (09) 968 8701
Email info@manukau.ac.nz
Website www.manukau.ac.nz
Diploma in Communication Studies — a full-time one-year course aimed at equipping students for roles such as editorial assistants, local newspaper journalists, introduction to public relations, etc, with modules on critical thinking, writing and communication, and media studies. A Certificate in Communication is also available.

Also offers a range of part-time courses concentrating on business report writing, professional and organisational writing and general business communication.

Massey University
Department of Communication and Journalism,
Private Box 756, Wellington. Tel (04) 801 5799 Fax (04) 801 2693
Email journalism@massey.ac.nz
Website www.massey.ac.nz
Graduate Diploma in Journalism — a full-time, one-year programme for graduates from a wide range of academic fields or for those with substantial life or work experience. This industry-supported course builds a firm foundation for careers in print journalism, radio and other media-related areas.
Graduate Diploma in Journalism Studies — offered extramurally and in Wellington. It is designed primarily for mid-career journalists but is also suitable for anyone with several years' experience in the communication industry. The course develops upgraded skills and higher levels of professional expertise and knowledge.
Bachelor of Communication — three year full-time degree programme (or equivalent) available at Auckland, Palmerston North and Wellington campuses or extramurally. Blend of business and creative disciplines. Option

in third year to major in journalism studies. Precursor to the Graduate Diploma in Journalism.

Nelson Marlborough Institute of Technology
Private Bag 19, Nelson.
Tel (03) 546 9175 Freephone 0800 4 career Fax (03) 546 2441
Email info@nmit.ac.nz
Website www.nmit.ac.nz
Diploma in Creative Writing — One year course offering modules on publishing and performance, poetry, fiction, non-fiction, introduction to creative writing and creating a specialist portfolio.
National Certificate in Film and TV —- Five month course which as well as covering practical aspects of production also includes scriptwriting and research.

Northtech
Private bag 9019, Raumanga Valley Road, Whangarei.
Tel (09) 430 5830 Fax (09) 430 5834
Email registry@northland.ac.nz
Website www.northland.ac.nz
All courses are delivered on-line through an interactive website. Students may take between one and four papers per semester. All prospective students are interviewed by phone.
Diploma of Applied Writing (level 5) —- Develops skills in a range of genres for children and adults. Options include writing picture books, History of literature and writing readers.
Diploma of Applied Writing (level 6) —- Collaborative projects, the business of writing and publishing. Options include feature writing, professional editing, novel writing.
Advanced Diploma in Creative Writing (level 7) — One-year course provides the framework for experienced writers to complete a major writing project — fiction or non-fiction — under the guidance of an established writer.
Diploma in Creative Writing — a two-year, full-time programme that introduces, develops and extends writing skills in a range of genres. It also gives professional knowledge of the business of writing. Students writing in Maori have editorial and translation support, and emerging Maori writers are considered a very necessary part of this programme. Topics include basic writing techniques, the history of literature generally (with a more detailed look at Maori, Pacific and Celtic culture and history), word processing, business, marketing, and the use of the Internet.

Southern Institute of Technology – Peter Arnett School of Journalism
Freepost 62685, Private Bag 90-114, Invercargill.
Tel (03) 218 2599 Freephone 0800 478 839 Fax (03) 214 4977

Email info@sit.ac.nz
Website www.sit.ac.nz
Bachelor of Applied Media and Arts (Journalism) — Three year full-time degree offering mixture of applied arts and practical training, including media law and ethics and writing for broadcast.
National Diploma in Journalism — the one-year diploma programme provides the essential skills required to secure employment in the newspaper industry, with a simulated newsroon environment and close links to the Southland Times and other newspapers.
Certificate in Radio and Journalism — One-year full-time broad introductory course including core journalism units covering print, radio and and television. Attention is given to the role of the media in society, with a focus on New Zealand's current economic, judicial and political structure. Written and interpersonal skills will also be a focus.
Certificate in Journalism —- One year full-time course covering basic journalism skills.
National Certificate in Journalism — Introductory 22 week (also available part-time) grounding in journalism, intended to provide necessary skills for entry into the National Diploma.

University of Auckland
Private Bag 92-019, Auckland.
Tel (09) 373 7999
Email postmaster@auckland.ac.nz
Master of Arts in Creative Writing — A one-year, full-time course offering the opportunity to complete a novel, collection of poetry or short fiction.
Undergraduate course in Creative Writing — These vary from year to year.
Centre for Continuing Education, Private Bag 92-019, Auckland.
Tel 0800 UNICONTED (0800 864 266) Fax (09) 373 7419
Email conted@auckland.ac.nz
Website www.cce.auckland.ac.nz
The Centre for Continuing Education offers a variety of writing courses throughout the year in addition to its January summer workshops. The tutors are well-known New Zealand writers, and a number of students who have attended Continuing Education classes have also become published writers. Courses covering all genres of writing are offered with daytime, evening or weekend options available. The classes cater for both beginning and experienced writers. Contact the Centre for Continuing Education for their current programme.

University of Canterbury
Private Bag 4800, Christchurch.
Tel (03) 366 7001

Email info@canterbury.ac.nz
Website www.canterbury.ac.nz
Graduate Diploma in Journalism — a one-year programme for graduates who intend to work in newspapers, magazines, radio, television, news and information for government and other agencies, or public relations. There is a strong emphasis on practical work. In addition to journalism skills, students study media law, the history and role of the news media, and the social and political background to the news. Analysis of the media and discussion of media issues and ethical questions are important elements in the course.

Victoria University of Wellington
International Institute of Modern Letters, P.O. Box 600, Wellington.
Tel (04) 463 6854 Fax (04) 463 6865
Email modernletters@vuw.ac.nz
Website www.vuw.ac.nz/modernletters
Master of Arts in Creative Writing — a one-year, full-time course specialising in either writing for the page or scriptwriting. The programme is directed by Professor Bill Manhire. Ken Duncum leads the scriptwriting stream.
Undergraduate Creative Writing workshops — limited to 12 students each and lasting 12 weeks. Workshops start in March, July and November, and usually include short fiction, poetry, creative non-fiction, children's writing, writing the landscape and creative non-fiction in the marketplace.

Waiariki Institute of Technology
Private Bag 3028, Rotorua.
Tel 0800 WAIRIKI (0800 924 274) Fax (07) 346 8768
Website www.wairiki.ac.nz
Diploma in Journalism — full-time, 18-month course designed to prepare graduates to work in print media. Emphasis on working in a multi-cultural environment. Incorporates the National Diploma in Journalism.
National Certificate in Journalism (Introductory) — Full-time 18-week course aimed at providing students with the relevant criteria for entry into the Diploma in Journalism.
Certificate of Creative Writing — A one-year part-time course which can be taken in modules including short story writing, poetry, children's writing, constructive editing, and creative non-fiction

Waikato Institute of Technology
Private Bag 3036, Waikato Mail Centre, Hamilton.
Tel 0800 2 WINTEC (0800 2 946 832) Fax (07) 858 0246
Email info@wintec.ac.nz
Website www.wintec.ac.nz

National Diploma in Journalism — a 32-week course with three-week work placement covering news writing and news gathering, court reporting, media law, Treaty issues, and feature writing.
Bachelor of Media Arts — a three-year full-time degree course which offers option of majors in print journalism, moving image (film and television) and public relations and advertising. In the first year, topics include writing and interpersonal skills. Students learn how to gather news, write for print, and edit copy; write for voice in radio, tape and edit interviews for radio news; shoot script, and edit for TV news.
Graduate Diploma in Communication — a 35-week course, covering professional studies in public relations, organisational communication, digital publishing, writing for the web, and advertising.
Certificate in Media Arts — a 20-week course that introduces study skills, written communications, interpersonal communication skills, and computer skills aimed at entry for further study at tertiary level.

Western Institute of Technology at Taranaki
Private Bag 2030, New Plymouth.
Tel 0800 948 896 Fax (06) 757 3235
Email info@witt.ac.nz
Website www.witt.ac.nz
National Diploma in Journalism (Print and Broadcasting) — a one-year, full-time course that aims to give students the skills they need for a career in newspaper or broadcast journalism. Course includes news reporting, writing for newspapers and radio, shorthand, keyboarding, interviewing, research, media law, numeracy, court and police reporting, sub-editing, local government reporting, media ethics, bicultural reporting and reporting diversity. Options include print journalism or broadcast journalism. Also available extramurally.

Whitireia Community Polytechnic
Private Bag 50-910, Porirua City.
Tel (04) 237 3100 Fax (04) 237 3101
Email info@whitireia.ac.nz
Website www.whitireia.ac.nz
Diploma in Publishing — full-time 32-week course in publishing, including practical experience and industry contacts. Planning and promoting a publication, and production from idea to printed publication. Also available online.
Bachelor of Applied Arts — Creative Writing. A three-year degree course with the aim of producing a major body of work with the help of mentors. First year explore a number of genres, and specialise in chosen field in the following years.
Graduate Diploma in Creative Writing — an advanced programme of

33 weeks allowing the opportunity to create a major body of work in fiction or non-fiction.
Certificate in desktop publishing for print and the web —hands-on introductory 20-week course focusing on the latest industry software with the opportunity to begin building a portfolio of work.
The National Diploma of Journalism and National Certificate in Journalism are also available

Correspondence courses

Courses by correspondence are also available for novice writers in New Zealand. Private correspondence schools offer a number of courses in this area, and their details are listed below.

New Zealand Institute of Business Studies
Principal, Brian Morris, P.O. Box 51-811, Auckland.
Tel 0800 801 994 or (09) 274 1917 Fax (09) 274 1933
Email registrar@nzibs.co.nz
Website www.nzibs.co.nz
A range of courses, including creative writing, freelance journalism, cartooning, book illustrating, travel writing, photography, writing stories for children, short stories, novels, plays and poetry, writing for the Internet, e-commerce, romance writing, crime writing, sports journalism, book editing, proofreading and publishing. Registered with NZQA. Free career counselling available.

Stotts Correspondence College
P.O. Box 30-990, Lower Hutt.
Tel (04) 567 6592 Freephone 0800 500 567 Fax (04) 569 3378
Offers courses in short story writing, novel writing, freelance journalism, scriptwriting, non-fiction book writing, poetry writing, writing for children and writing your autobiography.

The Writing School
P.O. Box 91-994, Auckland Mail Centre.
Tel 0800 771 010
Comprehensive Writing Course — covering article and short story writing.

Other courses

In addition to formal journalism courses, there are a number of short courses on writing held throughout New Zealand during the year — ranging from occasional workshops run by established writers, to writers' weeks, to evening classes on the basic elements of creative writing, to professional organisations that provide training in writing for business or pleasure.

It would be impractical to try to list the details of every course available in New Zealand — try your local library first, for information about courses in your area. Your nearest secondary school may also be able to help with details of evening classes. Local newspapers are always a good source of information about community institute courses, W.E.A. programmes and the like — keep an eye out early in the year, when most courses start to accept enrolments. You could also try entering 'writing course' or 'journalism' in a New Zealand search engine on the Internet.

Regional arts councils play an important role in fostering and encouraging local writers — your regional council may have information on local writing groups, writing courses and workshops, and may even support new talent through publication.

As writing tends to be a rather solitary occupation, one of the main benefits of courses, workshops and other programmes (for beginners and more advanced writers) is being in touch with like-minded people. They provide a forum for learning from other people, listening to, and developing your own ideas, and above all, gaining confidence and support in what you are doing.

APPENDIX A

Common Style Problems

Maori language style

1. Maori words should not be italicised in English text. 'She learnt Maori through the *rakau* method ...' should be amended to 'She learnt Maori through the rakau method ...'
2. Plurals should be avoided in a Maori/English context. 'The hunter was lost in the Ruahines ...' should be amended to read 'The hunter was lost in the Ruahine Ranges ...'. 'A large number of pukekos live in the swamp ...' should be amended to read 'A large number of pukeko live in the swamp ...'
3. Names of all tribes (iwi) and sub-tribes (hapu) should have their initial letters capitalised, e.g., Ngati Porou, Arawa, Ngai Tahu.
4. All proper names of Maori gods should have their initial letters capitalised, e.g., Rangi, Papa, Maui.
5. The names of Maori movements or religions should have their initial letters capitalised, e.g., Ratana Church, Hauhauism, Ringatu Church.
6. In Maori names with particles, e.g. Te, O, Nga, the initial letter of the particle should be capitalised unless the individual's preference is known to be otherwise.

The standard dictionary of the Maori language is: *A Dictionary of the Maori Language* (7th ed.), Williams, H. W. Wellington, GP Publications, 1992.

The Maori Language Commission (Te Taura Whiri i te Reo Maori) has some useful information regarding Maori language issues; visit the Commission's website at www.tetaurawhiri.govt.nz.

A free downloadable list of macrons for writers of Maori is available from www.dream-it.co.nz.

Bibliographic references

Any reference to a publication must contain enough information for the reader to identify and locate the work, if they so desire. There are several systems for referring to the publications within the text; the important thing is that a consistent form of reference be used throughout. The essential elements of any reference are the title; the edition number (if more than one); the author's name; the year of publication; and the place of publication. The name of the publisher can also be useful.

In a bibliography, it is usual to order and write these items in the following way:

PARSONS, J. F. *The New Zealand Writer's Handbook*. Auckland, David Bateman, 1996.

PARSONS, J. F. *The One That Got Away*. Wellington, Nelson Price Milburn, 1990.

Where two authors have collaborated on a text, both names should appear, without a comma between them, e.g., MICHENER, C. D. and BARKER, W. Where more than two authors have co-operated on a work, commas may be inserted between the names preceding the last author, e.g., WALLIS, D. M., BARRY, G. and TAHANA, W. If an editor is credited with a work, this should be noted by using (ed.) after his or her name.

Authorship by committee, government department or other organisation should be credited in the same way as that of an individual author.

Where details are unable to be found, e.g., a date is missing, probable details should be inserted within square brackets, '[ ]'. If probable details cannot be ascertained, use '[author unknown]' or similar.

The Harvard System

The Harvard System uses only surnames, dates, and (where necessary) page numbers within text; full references are given at the end of the chapter or book – 'in a recent guide to writing (Parsons, 1990), several conclusions ...'

There are several other systems used, with varying popularity. Whatever system you use, it must be followed consistently throughout a publication and include all the relevant information. Full details on standard bibliographic references for most New Zealand situations may be found in any of several editions of the Style Book, or in *The Writers' Handbook*, by M. Beazley and G. Marr, Hodder & Stoughton, Auckland, 1993.

Quotations

Short quotations, drawn from other publications, are usually enclosed in quotation marks, followed either by a reference to the publication or a mark indicating where the reference is to be found. If the quoted passage is substantial, other devices may be used to indicate that it is drawn from another publication. These include setting the quotation in smaller type, indenting the quoted matter, or setting the passage as solid matter, i.e., with little space between lines. Some rules which must be followed in any case are touched on below.

1. The quotation must use exactly the same words, spelling, style, etc., as the original.
2. If there are mistakes in the original, these may be indicated by using '[sic]' after the error.
3. Words cut from the original text should be shown as ellipses, e.g., 'The book was good reading ... and is to be recommended.'
4. Any additions made to the passage, such as explanatory notes, should be enclosed in square brackets.
5. All quoted sources should be acknowledged. Styles for acknowledgement vary — use one consistent method throughout your work.

Footnotes

Footnotes can be used where a quotation is being made or when a reference to another work, etc., is deemed necessary. At the place in the text where a reader is to be referred to a footnote, a raised number or symbol, such as a dagger, is placed; this is then reproduced at the bottom of the page, with the full reference. (Some publishers prefer to have all the footnotes at the end of the chapter or book.) All footnotes should be numbered consecutively within a chapter or book. As with bibliographic references, care should be taken to include full details of the publication in question, with the relevant page numbers, if necessary.

Where a publication is mentioned a number of times consecutively, the footnotes need not contain the full reference each time — you can simply put the author's name, followed by 'ibid.' — an abbreviation of the Latin for 'the same place'. Different page numbers will still need to be cited, however.

Copy editing for style

The following checklist covers most of the areas where inconsistencies and errors may arise within a manuscript.

- Is the manuscript complete?
- Are all pages numbered?
- Do all references to pages or other areas within the manuscript match actual positions?
- Are all references to other publications consistent in style and correct?
- Has material from other sources been properly acknowledged?
- Is house style concerning spelling, grammar, punctuation, referencing, etc. followed consistently?
- Are printer's instructions clear and unambiguous?

- Are proper names spelt and/or capitalised properly?
- Are quotations correct?
- Are foreign words spelt and used correctly?
- Are any additions to be made later noted in appropriate places?
- Does the writing contain anything defamatory or of dubious legal standing?

APPENDIX B

Marking Up

Outlined below is a system of correcting proofs and giving instructions to editors, typesetters and printers that is widely used both in New Zealand and overseas. As you will usually have the responsibility for proofreading your own galleys and page-proofs, you should become familiar with standard marking-up notation.

Printers' errors should be marked in red ink, and any alterations, corrected text, or further instructions should be written in blue or black. Notes and queries to the printer or typesetter should be labelled as such, and should be circled so that they will not be confused with the text.

For each instruction or correction, a mark in the text and in the margin should be made. Where a number of corrections need to be made in a line, divide the marks between the left and right margins, as evenly as you can, and in the right order. Make it clear what you mean when marking-up — corrections, especially at page-proof stage, are expensive to make.

Correction marks

Insert ⋏

The large cat swishd its tail. e/

Delete

There were ~~rather~~ dark clouds overhead.

Delete and close up

Dress was requested to be in/formal.

Leave as printed

It was a long, long time ago. stet

Use italics

Her faux pas was noticed by all. ital

Use even small capitals

The book referred to (Brown, R. 1988) s.c.

Use capitals

The government was clearly mistaken. cap

Use capitals and small capitals

Chapter 14: Geomorphology caps/s.c.

Use bold type

Caution should always be exercised. bold

Use lower case

CHOcolate wrappers littered the floor. l.c.

Use roman type

Climbing the steps *is* exhausting. roman

Wrong font

Wellington streets are hilly. w.f.

Character damaged

A pint of milk should be added. X

Use or insert characters above the line

In mathematics, 10 = 100.

Use or insert characters below the line (e.g. to indicate a reference)

In 1986, Kirkby stated the following:

Underline

This technique should not be used. u.l.

Delete space between letters

The k iwi is largely nocturnal.

Insert space

Meanwhile, theforest burned. #

Insert space between lines

\# > The sound of marching feet alerted him to the presence of others.

Reduce space between lines

less # (Use of slower films can often necessitate employing a

tripod. Tripods are generally available for less than $100.00.

Transpose

The ice-cream in melted the sunshine. trs.

Centre

NOTICE centre

Move text to right

In the gardens of Taranaki may be found several colourful imported species.

Move text to left

Marketing can often be broken into four essential areas.

Move text to indicated position.

[Further notes should be made by readers.] move

Take over characters or lines to next line, page, etc.

Several fine books exist on the art of t
ypography. take over

Take back characters or lines to next line, page, etc.

The volleyball match was inconclusi
ve. take back

Align vertically

Several of his antics were not to be
admired. First of all, there was his
inconsistent behaviour towards his
work. ||

Straighten lines

The pizza was ~~quickly~~ demolished.

New paragraph

In all these cases, there was no evidence. Nine times out of ten, juries are right. n.p.

No new paragraph

The noise from the room next door increased.

She stretched, and arose to confront the occupants. run on

Insert omitted copy

The terms are as follows: These terms are non-negotiable. out. see cop

Use or insert comma

At the time, in late August lambs were appearing.

Use or insert full stop

The artist reeked of tobacco His clothes were dishevelled.

Use or insert semicolon

The price includes airfares accommodation; and meals.

Use or insert colon

One thing had been forgotten the consequences

Use or insert question mark

"When" he asked.

Use or insert exclamation mark

"Of course" she retorted.

Insert parentheses

The kroner equivalent to $4.00 is a stable currency.

Insert en rule

... during the period 1940 45.

Insert em rule

Don't try it yourself unless you know what you are doing.

Insert apostrophe

Its no use complaining now.

Insert quotation marks

The weapon was no more than a piece of wood.

Insert ellipsis

And we all know where that can lead

Insert divider

The employer employee relationship was strained.

APPENDIX C

Glossary

As with most trades, printing has a language all of its own — a language that can be confusing and daunting to the uninitiated. The following glossary includes a selection of the more common terms used by those involved in the printing and publishing business.

A0, A1, A2, A3, A4, etc. — the series of standard paper sizes. A0 is one square metre (841 mm x 1189 mm); A1 is half that size; A2 half A1, etc. A4 paper is 210 mm x 297 mm.

Accent — a mark above or below a letter indicating a stress or sound (usually in foreign words).

Acetate — a transparent sheet of film placed over artwork for positioning or marking-up instructions.

Acknowledgement — a list of people or publications that have assisted the author in the preparation of a text.

Addendum — any material added to a book at a late stage, such as corrections or explanations.

Ampersand — the symbol '&' representing 'and'.

Appearing size — the actual size of a letter in a given font, as opposed to its point size (different fonts of the same point size can have different heights, widths, etc., on a printed page).

Appendix — any additional sections at the end of a book supplementing the main text.

Artwork — any drawings or other illustrations prepared to accompany the text.

Asterisk — the mark '*', usually noting some point in the text.

Backing up — printing on the back of a page which has already been printed on; also making a copy of a complete file (e.g., text) on a disk which is kept separately, in case the original is lost or accidentally deleted.

Back margin — the page margin nearest the spine.

Bibliography — a list of books and other relevant references, usually at the end of a book or article.
Blad — a promotional sample booklet, comprising pages from the original work.
Bled block — an illustration which runs to the edge of a page.
Block — an illustration, in relief, used in letterpress printing.
Blurb — a brief description of a book, usually appearing on the dust jacket.
Bold — heavy, thicker-faced type.
Bond paper — a heavier-grade paper, usually weighing about 80 grams per square metre.
Book proof — page proofs bound to appear as they will in the finished book.
Box — the lines enclosing text.
Brace — the connecting mark '{', indicating a number of lines leading into one.
Bromide — a light-sensitive paper used in photographic reproduction of illustrations, text or pages.
Caps — capital letters.
Caption — the title or explanation accompanying an illustration.
Case — the paper, cloth, or leather-covered cardboard forming part of a book's binding.
Casting off — calculating the number of lines of type a manuscript will run to, given a certain font and point size.
Catch line — a header used to identify galley proofs.
Close up — a printer's instruction meaning remove space between letters, words or lines.
Collate — put together, in the correct order, each section or page of a printing job.
Colophon — a logo or decorative symbol on a title page or book spine.
Column — a vertical area of type.
Compose — assemble type in groups of words.
Compositor — a person who sets type.
Condensed type — any type made up of thin, elongated characters.
Contents — a list of the main headings or chapters within a publication.
Copy — any text that the editor or printer receives for working on.
Corrigendum — a notice correcting a mistake from an earlier edition of a book.
Crop — cut down a drawing or photograph to a suitable size.
Dagger — the mark '[insert dagger]', used to indicate the presence of footnotes, etc.
Dis — unset type after printing.

Discount — the amount of the retail price of a publication that goes to the bookseller, retailer or wholesaler.

Display — set out the publication in the best possible way.

Dummy — a mock-up of a publication showing its dimensions.

Dust jacket — the removable wrapper around a hardcover book.

Dyeline — printer's final proof before printing. Same as ozalid.

Edition — all the copies of a publication printed using the same typesetting.

Em — a printer's unit of measurement, equal to the length of an 'm' in a particular font.

Em rule — a dash the length of an 'm' in a given font.

Embossed printing — a printing process resulting in raised print.

En — a printer's unit of measurement, half the length of an em.

End papers — the fly leaves at each end of a book, one of which is glued to the case.

Engraving — a method of reproducing illustrations using lines only, resulting in no gradations of black and white.

Epigraph — a quotation used in the preliminary pages of a book.

Errata — any errors within a book, noted in a list.

ESC — even-sized capitals.

Etching — using acid or tools to cut away sections of a plate to leave a clear image.

Extended type — any type made up of wider than usual letters.

Extent — the number of pages of a book.

Filler — any advertisement, illustration or other device used to occupy space on a page.

Fleuron — an ornamental flower-like character used for decoration on a page.

Fly leaf — the blank leaf at the front or back of a publication.

Folio — the page number of a book; or a publication made with sheets of paper folded only once.

Footnote — a note at the bottom of a page, explaining some part of the text.

Foreword — an introduction to a publication or its author, usually written by someone other than the author.

Format — the size and shape of a publication.

Font — a set of type designed with the same face and size.

Frontispiece — an illustration facing the title page.

Full-bound — a book bound entirely in cloth, leather, etc.

Full-out — no indentations.

Galley proof — an example of the text taken after initial typesetting is finished, but before pages have been formatted.

Glossary — an alphabetical list of technical or unfamiliar terms.

Half-bound — a book bound with cloth, leather, etc., only on the spine or corners.

Half-title — the short title appearing on the recto of the leaf preceding the title page. Also known as the bastard or false title.

Halftone — an illustration made from a photograph or shaded drawing, composed of dots of various sizes.

Hard copy — a printout of material held on computer disk.

Harvard System — a system of bibliographic reference which follows the form: surname, date and page number, within brackets, followed by a fuller description of the publication at the end of the chapter.

Hold-over matter — any text not used initially, but saved for possible future use.

House copies — any copies of a publication intended for use by the publisher.

House style — the rules of consistency used by different publishers within their publications.

Illustrations — any drawings, diagrams, photographs or other artwork used to accompany a piece of text.

Imposition — arranging pages on a large sheet of paper which, when printed and folded, will appear in the correct order.

Impression — all the copies of a publication printed at one time.

Imprint — the name or symbol of a publisher.

Indentation — setting text at a given space to the right of the left margin.

Index — an alphabetical list of names, places, etc., showing where they occur within a publication.

Inferior — any letters or numbers placed below the normal line of type.

Intaglio — a printing process in which type or illustrations are etched onto a plate.

Intertype — a machine which sets an entire line of type in a single piece of metal.

Introduction — author's preamble to the main body of a publication.

ISBN — International Standard Book Number (a number allocated to a book, which is unique to that book).

ISSN — International Standard Serial Number (a number allocated to a periodical, which is unique to that series of publications).

Italics — any typeface with letters sloping to the right.

Justify — setting text to have straight margins on both sides.

Layout — the design of a publication.

Lead — the space between lines.

Leaders — a series of dots, such as those which appear on a contents page, directing the reader's eye across the page.

Leaf — a sheet of paper in a publication.

Legend — another term for caption.

Letterpress printing — printing directly from blocks or type.

Line block — a black and white illustration using lines only, and without shading or gradations of tone.

Literals — any spelling, punctuation or textual errors introduced in typesetting.

Lithography — a printing process in which plates are chemically treated to accept ink only where desired.

Lower case — any letters that are not capitals.

Make up — arranging type into columns or pages of even length.

Manuscript — a typed or written original.

Margins — the space to either side, top and bottom of a page of text.

Measure — the width of a full line of type in either column or page form.

Octavo — a book in which the final pages are one-eighth the size of the unfolded paper sheet (actual dimensions may vary).

Offset — a printing process where an image is taken off a plate onto a cylinder and then transferred to paper.

Origination costs — the cost of bringing a publication to the point at which it is ready to be printed.

Orphan — the first line of a new paragraph occurring as the last line of a page.

Ozalid — printer's final proof before printing. Same as dyeline.

Page — one side of a leaf.

Page proof — a test printing, after text has been set in its final page form.

Paging — dividing text into page lengths.

Paste-up — positioning the final components of a page in their final arrangement, often by hand, using gum.

Photogravure — a printing process in which plates are etched by photographic means.

Pica — a measure of type size, one-sixth of an inch, or the size of typewritten letters, ten to an inch.

Plate — a metal surface used for printing; an illustration on one side only of an inserted leaf.

Point — a measure of type size, a multiple of one-twelfth of a pica.

Preface — the section of a publication where the author addresses the reader, usually backgrounding the book or its preparation, etc.

Preliminary matter — anything preceding the main body of text, such as introductions, prefaces, etc.

Proof — a trial printing.

Quarto — a book where the final pages are one-quarter the size of the unfolded paper sheet (actual dimensions may vary).

Range — align text (left, right, horizontally, etc.)

Recto — a right-hand page.
Register — the alignment of pages or colours within a publication.
Returns and frees — any books given away as complimentary copies, for reviews, returned from booksellers or destroyed. (On average, 15% of hardcovers and 25% of paperbacks end up as returns and frees.)
Reverse out — white print on a coloured background.
Roman — any normal, upright typeface.
Rotary machine — a printing press with cylindrical plates.
Rules — any printed lines on a page.
Saddle stitch — a binding method, using wire or thread stitched through the back to the middle of folded paper.
Sans serif — a typeface without the short cross-lines that often appear at the ends of letters.
Scoring — creasing a sheet of paper.
Screen — a block of a different colour or shading on a page.
Serif — the short cross-line at the end of the strokes of letters.
Show-through — the degree to which printing on one side of paper can be seen from the other side, due to paper quality.
Side stapling — stapling pages down the left-hand side.
Signature — a folded and printed sheet of paper which contains a number of pages in order.
Slug — a line of type in one piece of metal.
Soft copy — any text stored on computer disk.
Solid matter — any type without spacing between the lines.
Spot colour — a single colour added in printing.
Standing type — any type which is stored for future use.
Stet — a printer's instruction, meaning 'leave as is'.
Superior — any letter or number printed above the normal line of text.
Title verso — the reverse of the title page, sometimes known as the bibliographic page, containing copyright information, ISBN, and technical details about the book.
Transpose — to shift letters, lines, paragraphs, etc., from one place to another.
Type face — the design of letters or numbers.
Upper case — capitals.
Verso — a left-hand page.
White — any area of a page where nothing is printed.
Whiting out — spacing out lines of type.
Widow — the last line of a paragraph appearing as the first line of a new page.
Wrong font — a printer's instruction, indicating a letter or number of the wrong design has been used.

Index